Clock In

Clock In

No-BS Advice for Getting Ahead in Your Career (Without Losing Your Mind)

Emily Durham

TARCHER
an imprint of Penguin Random House
New York

t

Tarcher
an imprint of Penguin Random House LLC
1745 Broadway, New York, NY 10019
penguinrandomhouse.com

Book design by Shannon Nicole Plunkett

LIBRARY OF CONGRESS CATALOGING-IN-PUBLICATION DATA
has been applied for.

Hardcover ISBN: 9798217176915
Ebook ISBN: 9798217176922

Printed in the United States of America
1st Printing

The authorized representative in the EU for product safety and compliance is Penguin Random House Ireland, Morrison Chambers, 32 Nassau Street, Dublin D02 YH68, Ireland, https://eu-contact.penguin.ie.

This book is dedicated to everyone who has invited me on their career journey. Thank you for having me in your life and on your bookshelf. I love you.

CONTENTS

INTRODUCTION

LET'S GET STARTED

Welcome. If you're reading this, I'm guessing your dad isn't a CEO. You didn't strike it rich at the casino. There's no trust fund with your name on it. So, much like me, you started picking up self-help books designed to empower you in your career and, you know, help you get your shit together—only to realize most of these books are written by someone who already has money. The kind of person who gives advice like "Want a raise? Just ask for it!" The kind of person who probably hasn't had to apply for a job in a really long time.

I aspire to be that rich and oblivious someday, but for now, I'm just a good old-fashioned corporate girl, who worked as a recruiter for ten-plus years. I've been responsible for designing and delivering international recruitment strategies for some of the largest companies in the world, meaning I help those companies attract top talent for their open positions. I've made a career out of recruiting for global top employers and creating career-development content for an audience of over three million people, becoming one of the most recognized online thought leaders in the space.

Do I sound cocky? By the end of this book, you'll be feeling cocky, too. You'll have access to the industry secrets that were previously gatekept and the confidence to do something about it. You'll be less anxious about where your career is and where it's going.

You'll be able to define and reach your goals without that nagging voice in your head telling you that you're not good enough. You're going to be your own hype person.

This is not the fluffy, corporate book that your professor or boss is going to recommend. This book is about how to kick ass, not kiss it. I'm not going to have you manifest your "dream job" (those are bullshit, by the way, but we'll talk about that later). I'm not going to have you journal every day, either. This book is your end-to-end, no-bullshit guide to identifying, pursuing, and excelling in your career as a not-yet-rich bitch. It's tactical, practical, and interactive (get ready to work a little).

Whether you're just starting your career or simply looking for practical tools to develop your corporate confidence, you're in the right place. Your dad may not be a CEO, but your big sister Em is here to help you get ahead at work—without getting all worked up. Let's get into it.

CHAPTER 1

WAKE UP, THE DREAM ISN'T YOURS

I have a feeling the person who first said, "If you love your job, you'll never work a day in your life" is the same person who said, "You'll find love when you least expect it." So far, they're 0 for 2.

Think back to the first time someone asked you, "What do you want to be when you grow up?" You were probably five or six years old, sitting in a classroom with a well-intentioned teacher asking you to draw a picture of your *dream job* on construction paper. You could barely tie your shoes, and yet they were asking you to draw pictures of taxable activities. Very capitalism coded.

"What do you want to be when you grow up?"

"What are you going to study?"

"What are your career goals?"

All valid questions . . . for people who have fully developed frontal lobes. *Sigh.*

These same questions likely echoed in high school when suddenly you were seventeen and feeling the pressure to pick the perfect university program to help you land your dream job. If you didn't pick the right major, it seemed, your whole life would be thrown off track. You'd be working in the wrong field, miserable and making no money, unable to afford a place to live or a family.

Teenage you—the same you who likely stole beers from your parents' fridge and lied about where you were going with your friends—was responsible for making a life-altering decision. A roughly $100,000 decision at that. You couldn't drive, vote, or order a martini, but you were somehow expected to have the entirety of your professional life mapped out.

Dare I say we're a little too comfortable asking kids to dream of labor?

WAKING UP FROM THE DREAM

Listen, I'm not going to get philosophical on your ass in every chapter, but you need to hear this. By the end of this book, you're going to feel completely equipped to navigate and redirect your career a million times over. But first, you'll need to emotionally detach from the process, otherwise it's going to eat you alive.

This starts with understanding that the "dream job" is just that: a dream. It doesn't actually exist.

Why is that? For one thing, the aspirations we dream up early in life are limited by our youth and lack of experience, and they often don't correspond with the way our careers actually turn out. In fact, a startling 50 percent of recent college grads are working in fields that don't use their degrees.

As a kid, when you were asked about your career aspirations, where did your answer come from? The careers we dream of are the careers we know exist and that we believe we have access to. Naturally as a seven-year-old, you aren't consciously processing these factors, but they are still very much at play.

Children's career ambitions are molded by what they see. For example, I knew my dad worked in sales, my mom worked in insurance, and most of the women I saw on TV worked in fashion or were stay-at-home moms. I also really liked my grade 4 teacher. She was cool. So here were the career options I could imagine:

- Actress
- Sales
- Full-time mom
- Fashion designer
- Fashion model
- Teacher

(Working in insurance was never on the list, even back then. Sorry, Mom.)

Chances are the dream job you had as a child was informed by your environment, too. And chances are the dream job you aspired to have as a young adult was, at least a little bit, informed by your childhood dream job or self-beliefs. It's all connected, and we can't get ahead until we disconnect.

Humor me. Make a list of the jobs you were interested in as a child, and then the jobs you were aiming to enter in high school and college. Notice any patterns? What beliefs did you hold about your skills and abilities?

Let's unpack that.

Not to state the obvious, but the jobs on your list were all jobs that you knew existed as a kid because you had exposure to them through your family, friends, or media. If a job was more obscure or unglamorous, you probably hadn't heard of it: Bob the Actuary or Bob the Warehouse Project Manager doesn't have quite the same ring as Bob the Builder. Other times, young people might know a career path exists but are discouraged from exploring it because of family expectations and pressures to pursue certain jobs. (I think my cousins are still disappointed I'm not a lawyer.)

MANUFACTURED DREAMS

My point is: Our environment shapes our career ambitions and the confidence we have to pursue them. One of the best examples of this is the relative lack of women in fields related to STEM (science, technology, engineering, and math). In 2024, only about

30 percent of people working in STEM jobs were women, even though women, of course, represent about 50 percent of the population.

When they hear this statistic, some people think, *Clearly, women just don't want to work in those fields.* Or worse: *Women are bad at STEM.* But it isn't as simple as that.

In fact, it isn't simple at all. Because when we look at the impact of stereotypes, representation, support, and access, it becomes clear that succeeding in your career is not as simple as following your "dreams."

STEREOTYPE THREAT

Our dreams for our future start with our self-concept from an early age, even as early as elementary and middle school. Studies suggest that about 74 percent of middle-school girls have an interest in STEM subjects but that this number significantly drops when they reach high school. Why? For starters, there is a stereotype that math and science are inherently masculine and that boys are naturally better at these things. These stereotypes impact the way young girls see themselves at such a formative age that it directly impacts their academic performance.

A study conducted by UCLA and Xiamen University aimed to challenge the belief that boys are better than girls at math across eight thousand middle-school students in China. It found that middle-school girls *typically* scored better than boys on a math test both groups were given. (Slay.) However, the higher the proportion of students who believed that boys were better at math, the worse the girls performed on the test.

This phenomenon is known as *stereotype threat*. It tells us that how well girls tend to do in STEM is directly related to how well they *believe* they can do. Similarly, we only chase careers we think we will succeed in. See where I'm going? If we believe from a young age that we can't be good at certain jobs, those career dreams will be dead before we even imagine them.

THE IMPORTANCE OF REPRESENTATION

In addition to our exposure to stereotypes, how much we believe we can accomplish is often limited by what we have seen others accomplish. For this, our main sources of influence are our parents and the media.

A Microsoft study shows that when young women know a woman in STEM, they're 20 percent more likely to "feel empowered by STEM activities." But only roughly 8 percent of the STEM workforce in 1970 were women. Eight percent! Statistically speaking, most of our grandmas, moms, and aunts were not in STEM. This means *most* young girls are less likely to feel capable of occupying a career in STEM and, even if they were interested, wouldn't know how to get there.

We also know the media doesn't always paint the most dynamic picture of women in the workforce, especially if you go back to the stuff we grew up with in the '90s and early 2000s (let alone before that). And as they grow older, these girls will see that most STEM professors are men. Most hiring managers in STEM are men. If they don't see people who look like them in STEM roles, why would they think they're capable of occupying those roles? Especially if most of their experience with STEM consists of being told they aren't naturally skilled at it? Ouch.

The difference between girls' and boys' ability to dream of STEM careers has ramifications in the real world. Boys end up with more access to education, training, and career opportunities (and may not understand the hurdles a young woman may have to overcome). A male new grad may very well have four years of tech internship experience, while his female counterpart may have only one—or none at all. Not because she isn't great but because she had to spend her time breaking down doors, not coding on the other side of them.

FACING HOSTILITY

When women do break down the doors and enter STEM careers, they're not always given a warm welcome. In 2015, platform engineer Isis Anchalee (formerly Isis Wenger) was featured in a recruitment marketing campaign for her company. In theory, this is exactly the kind of effort we need to show girls and young women that they can have STEM careers. In practice, well . . . you may need a coffee, or something stronger, for this one.

Wenger went viral, but the bad kind of viral. Thousands of people online claimed she was a "hired model" and was "too feminine and hot" to be an engineer. In response, Wenger posted a photo of herself holding a sign that read *#ILookLikeAnEngineer* to challenge the notion of what an engineer looked like. This hashtag eventually trended on social media and became the push for a global movement to challenge stereotypes of who can be an engineer.

This is a very public example of what waits for women on the other side of the door (and an example of how the stereotypes and lack of representation we previously discussed are perpetuated). But it's not at all unique. Many studies also show that women in STEM are often not taken as seriously as their male counterparts and are significantly more likely to experience workplace discrimination, sexism, and outright harassment. And the intersections of race, sexuality, ability, and gender can significantly worsen the impacts of these experiences. A dream job can quickly become a nightmare.

A DIFFERENT DREAM

What's my larger point here? Our dreams for our careers aren't ours alone. Whether it's something as simple as never having heard of a marketing manager or as complex as trying to enter a STEM field as a woman, our ideas about our dream jobs are largely shaped by the people and media around us.

Knowing that, what if we gave ourselves permission to detach all our hopes and dreams from our jobs? To stop thinking that what we do for work is an inherent part of who we are? Yes, work is important. But it isn't everything. The vast majority of us won't be on our deathbed wishing we could work another shift. You may love your job, but—much like my ex-boyfriend—it isn't going to love you back.

Given that your dream job isn't baked into your DNA, what if we took a minute to challenge the idea of what we thought we wanted and examine whether you're on the right path?

Before you panic: If you're studying or working in your dream industry, I love that for you. The best thing you'll ever do for your career is follow your passion. But that only works if you give yourself permission to change your passion and path as needed. I'm a big believer in checking in with yourself every year by saying, "Self, am I still doing what I want?" So, whether you're starting from scratch on your career or just checking in with yourself, let's forget the dreams and ask ourselves where we really want to be.

Your Hit List

Get out a pen and paper (or your iPad if you're an iPad kid). In this exercise, you're going to write the formula for your dream job—or, more accurately, your awake job. (It doesn't sound as sexy, but you'll enjoy it more.)

1. *Start by writing a list of your natural strengths, such as public speaking, selling, or people skills. Write down as many as you can think of. If you're not sure you're "good enough" at a given skill to add it to this list, ask yourself why. What if you gave yourself a chance to be good at it?*

What if you told yourself that you could be? Add a couple more to the list—don't be modest! Next, circle the skills on the list you actually enjoy (or at least, enjoy enough if you're being paid to do them). This is called your Hit List.

2. *In another list, write down the things you are legitimately bad at and/or really dislike. If you're not great at something, but you generally like it, there's hope of improving—that's not what this list is for. This list is for stuff you truly don't want to do in a job. This is called your Shit List.*

3. *Make a third and final list of your must-haves when it comes to work. Is a traditional nine-to-five better or worse for you? How important is work-life balance? Pay? Vacation? This is your Good Fit List.*

4. *Now open up your browser and search "job with" plus a couple of the circled skills on your Hit List. For example, when I search "jobs with people skills and public speaking," here are some of the results I get:*

    - *Tour guide*
    - *Teacher*
    - *Reporter*
    - *Sales representative*
    - *Public relations manager*
    - *Public speaking coach*
    - *Curator*
    - *Moderator*

5. *Write all the jobs down and then vet them by looking up job postings for each. For example, I might look up sales representative jobs in Toronto to see how many jobs are posted, what the average salary looks like for these roles, if the job descriptions actually sound interesting, and if the industries offering these jobs are up my alley. I may also go on social media to watch videos from sales*

representatives vlogging their day or talking about their experience, to get a better sense of whether the job is the right fit for me.

6. *As you do this research, evaluate how well each posting fits with your Hit List, Shit List, and Good Fit List. You should have a sense of what the job requirements are, what the responsibilities are, how much you can expect to be paid, what kinds of industries hire for this role, and whether there are many or very few opportunities available. If these core factors seem aligned with what you want, great! That means this is one of potentially several viable career paths you can consider as you continue reading this book!*

VPL: VALIDATION, PURPOSE, LIFESTYLE

What you want in your career has largely been shaped by your environment, and there's nothing wrong with that. But there is so much power in understanding that what we have always wanted and what we will want in the future may evolve alongside our environment, circumstances, and sense of self. And there's even more power in bringing awareness to the self-beliefs we hold that were shaped by our childhood—and giving ourselves the chance to challenge them.

The worst thing you can do is be married to a path that one day may no longer be the path you want. If you feel chained, you won't allow yourself to change.

Your career will get significantly less stressful once you detach your sense of self from your work. Because as much as our careers feel like an integral part of who we *are*, they're actually just what we *do*. Although they influence us as people, they aren't who we are at our core.

The reason I spend so much time emphasizing the importance of emotionally detaching from work is (a) for your mental health and (b) because love kind of makes us stupid. (Oh my God, am I describing my dating life? Wrong book!) But this next section is going to help you get smart again.

So. If the dream job isn't real . . . what have you been dreaming of, really?

This is a question I often ask my career-coaching clients. The conversations all tend to go the same way. They share a defined career goal or job they're targeting (yay). I ask them, "What about this job is interesting to you?" Usually, they share some responsibilities listed on the job description that they're good at and generally enjoy. Sometimes they share an interest they have in the company, or the desire for more pay or better work-life balance.

All of these are valid reasons for dreaming of a job. And all of these reasons are related to three core needs that all people have: validation, purpose, and a lifestyle we enjoy. We can combine these needs into one *Jersey Shore*–style term: *VPL*.

Because we've been conditioned to dream of labor (literally, gross), we think we're targeting a job alone, when the reality is that most of us are targeting these three core needs, and the job is just how we plan to get there. Recognizing the difference can help you do things like:

- Pivot and change your career path when a job no longer fulfills your needs. You won't experience guilt over not feeling attached to a "dream job" if you're attached to VPL.

- Expand the roles you're open to, because you're not married to a job title—you're married to VPL.

- Kickstart your job search and career in a way that is always backed by your VPL.

If you identify the type of job that feels like a good fit for you, and combine that with a deeper understanding of your unique VPL, you'll be equipped to make more educated career decisions, experience less burnout, and ultimately give yourself permission to change your mind as your VPL evolves.

Humans naturally enjoy tasks that we excel at. (This is why I love complaining—it just comes naturally to me.) Doing things that come easily to us reinforces our belief that we're capable, smart, and competent. The more we do things we're good at, the more confident we feel, both in that specific area and in our relationship to ourselves in general.

On the flip side of this, many of us grow to dislike tasks that we perceive ourselves to be bad at. Do you actually hate math, or does it just not come easily to you? Do you actually dislike cooking, or do your dishes not turn out very tasty? This tells us that, to an extent, we look for jobs that make us feel competent. It makes sense. Why would we want to spend eight hours a day being told or shown that we aren't great at something?

We've all been there. For me, it was working at my local Starbucks in high school, where I couldn't bear the weight of the coffee pots that we were required to carry during our shifts. The two twigs I called arms would begin to shake and eventually drop the containers at least once a shift, spilling liters of dark roast over the counters. I went home from every shift feeling like an absolute idiot.

So what did I do? I decided to hit the gym daily, doing forty-pound dumbbell curls until I became the most physically in-shape employee on record.

If you believed that, thank you. The reality was my ass got fired.

Well, the separation was mutual. Really, I saw a termination coming and jumped ship before they could can me. It really was such a relief. I no longer had to feel like an incompetent loser every single shift. Being bad at that job really took a bite out of my confidence overall. But pivoting from that to a retail job I was great at really shifted my perspective both on my skills and capabilities.

Why? Because of VPL: validation, purpose, lifestyle.

- Validation. The first core need that we look to satisfy at work is validation. Most people want to work a job they're good at so they can feel validated through positive career outcomes. If you've ever been in a job or a class you sucked at, compare how you felt about yourself there with how you felt in spaces you generally excelled in. It's like night and day. You carried yourself differently, spoke differently, and were on the opposite end of the anxiety spectrum.

- Purpose. Humans crave purpose. The American Psychiatric Association found that 58 percent of young adults felt they lacked meaning or purpose in their lives, which was directly related to having significantly worse mental health and life satisfaction. Purpose can come in many forms, but in our money-hungry world, we're often told that our purpose comes from our careers. In interviews, when you're asked, "Why do you want to work here?," simply saying, "Because I need the money" is never enough. Instead, we're coached to share how the company's mission aligns with our own, how we want to contribute to their organizational goals. How we want them to give us purpose. So whether we realize it or not, when we look for jobs, we also look for purpose.

- Lifestyle. This one isn't shocking. We look for jobs to fund and support our lifestyles. This means your job should support your financial needs for things like travel, housing, dining, or online shopping. Lifestyle also includes the hours you work, where you work them from, and the culture of your industry. This is arguably the most significant factor, because no matter how shiny and impressive a job may be, if it can't support your lifestyle, you'll want to leave sooner than later.

To be clear, the elements of VPL are all *good* things. Aiming to have validation, purpose, and a lifestyle you enjoy is an incredible anchor that helps you make intentional decisions in your career. You just need to be aware of them so that you don't fool yourself into believing the core source of satisfaction is your career alone.

Talking this through with my clients usually leads to some kind of an aha moment. Not because their career ambitions have changed or should change—they shouldn't. The breakthrough comes from realizing where their career ambitions are coming from and giving each ingredient a name.

Suddenly it becomes less about searching for a dream job and more about curating a dream life that is supported by a really good job. Suddenly the work we do or are searching for isn't a core part of who we are, it's simply a component of a life we're building for ourselves.

The truth is you can get your VPL needs met with work, school, friends, family, hobbies, and just about anything in between. You get to decide what fuels your VPL . . . and it doesn't always have to be a career. Sometimes we don't desire a particular career; we just desire a job we like that can fund a life we love. And that's totally cool. Other times, a career *is* a core driver of VPL, and that's totally valid, too. The point is that just as your life and needs change, so can the ways you fill your VPL cup. Understanding this can relieve the pressure of the need to have a "perfect career path" and can help you prioritize what matters most to you in any season of life.

YOUR JOB IS JUST NOT THAT INTO YOU

Our job isn't a singular thing that will fix all of our woes. And it shouldn't be powerful enough to spoil our weekends. It's not everything.

Guys, it's literally just a job.

So if our true dream is to achieve personal satisfaction through validation, purpose, and lifestyle, how can we hack the equation so that work isn't the only variable? (So math queen of me. Damn, am I a woman in STEM?) Because when work is the only variable, it has the power to make us feel like shit when we encounter mean bosses, organizational changes, and, of course, layoffs.

Remember, it's OK to love your job. But it's important to understand where the love is coming from so it doesn't break your heart.

Ultimately, love makes us kind of stupid. It gives us rose-colored glasses that make it difficult to see a situation for what it is. Like when you tell yourself the cutie you've been going on dates with isn't ghosting you; they're just not texting you because they have a healthy relationship with technology and don't spend all day on their phone! They really like you, they just aren't ready for a relationship! See what I'm saying? It makes us kind of silly.

The challenge with loving your job or seeking a job that you love is that *your job will never love you back*. Like, ever. Much like the date who ghosts you, your job is just not that into you. And much like in a toxic relationship, you can't untie your identity from your job until you realize that.

Of course, companies want us to think they love us. (How else will they take advantage of us?) Almost every company has a careers page on their website where they boast about their corporate values and social responsibility initiatives alongside their job postings. Go on any company's careers website and count how many times you read nonsense like:

"We put our people first."

"People are at the center of what we do."

"We have an award-winning culture."

"We operate with integrity."

"Join our family."

Companies love to use emotionally charged, community-building language to trick candidates and employees into thinking their core desires will be met there. "We're not like the other corporations! We really care about you!" This language is repeated ad nauseam in the interview process, where recruiters gush about the incredible corporate culture; during onboarding, where you're told that you've really made an incredible decision for your career; and of course at company-wide meetings and events, because "we aren't just a company, we're a family." (The kind of family that needs therapy, but I digress.)

Every company wants you to think they're not like those other companies—they're the good guys. Reality check: No company is a "good guy." But companies know that in order to attract and keep you, they need you to believe they care.

Now, as a former recruiter, I do think it's important to call out that recruiters are people, too. People who genuinely want to see you shine and are invested in your career. I have cried tears of joy on the phone with candidates when they signed a job offer that has changed their life. I have celebrated career wins with my recruiter friends when their recent hire gets promoted. So I'm not trying to come across as anti-recruiter. This is anti–corporate culture. This book is designed to help you navigate the murky job market and prepare for when companies try to take advantage of you.

YOUR JOB IS LOVE-BOMBING YOU

Have you heard of "love-bombing"? In short, it's when someone tries to shower you with love, affection, and praise very early on in a relationship so that you feel valued and ultimately loyal to them. Eventually, once the love bomber gets what they want (your unwavering devotion), they pull back and take away the positive affirmations and attentiveness they used to hook you. The emotionally intelligent, kind, and thoughtful person you thought was committed to you is suddenly someone who hardly replies to your texts (and may even become downright toxic).

Companies kind of do the same thing. They know humans have a desire to feel valued, so what do they do? They manufacture a sense of belonging in exchange for our loyalty. When we interview for a company and even in the early months of us working there, we're effectively being love-bombed.

Recruiters praise the company culture endlessly during the interview process, boasting about the unique work and incredible people. Remember, they aren't like the other companies; they're *different.* You want something different. The offer is solid. You take the job.

On your first day of work, you attend orientation, where a chipper HR representative greets you with a bag of company swag. Water bottles, T-shirts—you've hit the corporate-branded-items lottery. This day rocks!

You hear about the endless opportunities to grow at this company, the open and supportive leadership team and of course, the *fun* office culture. In each team meeting, your boss speaks about the VP of your department like she's Beyoncé. The VP speaks about the shareholders as if she were personally on the hook for paying their dividends. The office chatter is riddled with a familiar language: "I care so much about my product." "Our team cares so much about what we're doing." "My hope for the company is . . ."

They say if you live in Paris for a few months, you're bound to pick up some French. Well, I say if you work at a company for a few months, you're bound to start picking up on their corporate language. Slowly, you start to speak using "we" language when talking about the company. "We had such a good quarter." "We just launched a new product." "Our customers are so happy."

And although it's not a bad thing to care about the work you do and the impact it has on customers and community, it is a bad thing when you begin to see yourself as one with the company. You are no longer two separate entities. You are a *we.* The love-bombing worked; they've got you hooked. You feel like part of the corporate family.

There is so much value in having a workplace that fosters a

shared sense of purpose and community. In fact, Boston Consulting Group conducted a study that found organizations that foster an inclusive and community-based culture have happier and more productive employees. So feeling connected to the work you do is a great thing. But too much of this feeling can make it hard to separate who you are generally versus who you are at work—especially given the fact that usually this feeling is entirely disingenuous. Your employer *says* everyone is one big happy family (barf), but the reality is everyone is overworked and underpaid.

When we hear (emphasis on *hear*, because what evidence have you really *seen*?) that our company is the "good guys," we identify ourselves as one of them. *We* are the good guys.

That's how organizational identification—the feeling of personally identifying with your job—is born. And surprise! It's actually twins, because along with organizational identification comes blind company loyalty. This dynamic of blind loyalty is perhaps most obvious in the corporate world, but you can see it play out in every type of job there is, from retail to entertainment to small businesses with only a few employees.

At first, you'll notice the heightened sense of community gives you a way to bond with your coworkers, a sense of common interest. Then you start to feel personally responsible for the outcomes of your team and then the overall business. Next, you'll feel awfully anxious every time you make a mistake, because you don't want to let your corporate family down. Your anxiety about work seems to rise, and you're more willing to skip breaks and to work overtime because you care that much. Sound familiar?

"OK, so I feel connected to my company," you may be saying. "What's the big deal?" The big deal is there's a very thin line between connected and tethered, sister.

The issue with believing the positive stories a company sells you is threefold: They heighten your sense of responsibility and anxiety, the stories usually aren't true, and your job can't love you back.

Let's take a closer look at each factor.

A HEIGHTENED SENSE OF RESPONSIBILITY AND ANXIETY

Dozens of my clients come to me with the same experience: *Emily, every time I send an email with a typo in it, I feel a rush of anxiety through my body. My heart sinks, and it feels like the world is shaking underneath me. I immediately think that I'm an idiot and wonder how I could make such a silly mistake. No one else seems to make as many mistakes as I do.*

Typos in emails, presentations that didn't go to plan, being two minutes late to a meeting. The list of tiny blunders that feel like boulders goes on and on. When you're in it, you may logically understand that the mistake is small and rather meaningless, but trying to talk yourself off of the emotional cliff with logic rarely works. Especially not when you're emotionally attached to *the company.*

Going back to my first job out of university, I vividly remember getting on the subway at Toronto's King Station in the middle of July after a long day of being a recruitment coordinator at a large Canadian bank. Toronto summers are hot, sticky, and, when you're on the subway during rush hour, viscerally smelly. I stepped onto the train with my laptop bag in hand, battling the heat—and immediately started crying. Dozens of people were looking at me like I had lost my marbles.

The reason for my public breakdown? I had forwarded an email to the wrong Cathy. One Cathy was an executive assistant, and one was an executive. I'd sent a booking request to a VP, not her EA. A cardinal sin. Surely, this would stick with me forever. I sat with the same line of thinking: *I am such an idiot. Everyone is going to think I'm so stupid. How could I do this?*

I sobbed the entire way home, where I fell into my mom's arms. She repeated the same thing she always did: "None of this will matter in ten years." She was right. The time has passed, and I am happy to report the bank didn't cut off my thumbs for a misplaced email. In fact, no one really cared. And though there are toxic bosses in this world who would care, most workplaces wouldn't. So why did I feel so upset about it?

Subconsciously, some of the anxiety we feel about not being perfect at work comes from the fact that we don't want to let our boss and organization down. We don't want to be a disappointment.

When we believe the narrative that our companies are the good guys, we feel a sense of moral obligation to them. We think:

"They treat me well, so I need to perform well."

"They gave me a chance in this role, and I can't let them down."

"My boss thinks the world of me—I don't want to fail them."

And when we inevitably "fail" by making a human mistake, it begins to feel like a moral failing. Like we've let down a close friend. We look at the company as if it were a person we work with. But the employees and the company are two separate entities. One has the power to fire you, and the other doesn't. Your boss may be a good guy, but the company that employs both of you frankly doesn't give a shit, even when they say they do.

Your career journey will never be healthy until you learn how to detach from this dynamic. If you're not there yet, don't worry, we'll get there.

THE STORIES AREN'T TRUE

"At Definitely Not an Evil Conglomerate, Inc., we care about our people. We put our people first. They're at the center of what we do," says every company, ever. But is it actually true?

Let's look at one notable example. When the COVID-19 pandemic hit in 2020 and a huge portion of the population started working from home, the competition for talent fundamentally changed. Companies no longer had to exclusively recruit candidates who were close to their offices. In a remote world, the talent pool became global. At the same time, we started to see the Great Resignation, a fascinating period of time in which employees were sick of being treated like crap at the height of a global pandemic and opted to leave their jobs. This opened up the door for tech giants to offer high-paying remote jobs where workers would supposedly be treated well as part of a thriving corporate culture. The surge in hiring created a sense of optimism in an otherwise pretty awful time. (How awful? I was making sourdough. That's how you know it was bad.)

So in 2023, when the world slowly started to return to some degree of normal, imagine the collective gasp that was let out when we started to see news that our loving, worker-friendly tech companies were conducting mass layoffs. And not just layoffs, but the kind of layoffs where you tell people they've lost their jobs over Zoom with no notice. I know you saw those viral videos. Surely these were not the same companies that were so invested in job creation three short years ago. Surely they wouldn't be laying off women on maternity leave without so much as a phone call. They were the good guys, remember?

Or were they? The same companies who were bragging about their progressive diversity, equity, and inclusion initiatives at the height of the racial justice movement in 2020 are the same ones who gladly dismantled these programs in 2025.

The story your company tells you and the public is whichever story is selling at that moment in time. Assume 80 percent of what you hear is performative and has ulterior motives.

YOUR COMPANY CAN'T LOVE YOU BACK

This is not to say that your company is inherently evil. Or that your boss is a monster. What I'm saying is: Your company can't love you back.

It's not an easy pill to swallow, mostly because you may really like your coworkers or even your boss. The people may be great. The vibes may be vibing. But say it with me: The people who make up the company are not the company.

The compliment your boss gave you is not a compliment from the company. It's a compliment from your boss.

The work bestie you made wasn't birthed by the company. You two just happened to meet there.

The promotion you received wasn't from the company. It was from the people who recognized your value and put you through the promotion process.

A company is only as good as its people, true. But a company is not inherently good. Companies operate with one goal in mind: to make money. In times of economic challenge, tech giants were not concerned with laying off thousands of employees. They didn't lose sleep over creating thousands of jobs during a global pandemic just to axe them "upon further reflection." No. They realized they weren't hitting financial goals. They acted in the interest of the organization's bottom line. Spoiler: You are never something they consider.

Even though you may love your boss, love the work you do, and feel genuinely cared for, it isn't the company that's caring for you. It's the people they hired.

When people are impacted by a layoff or get fired, you'll usually hear them say things like: "I can't believe this happened, after everything I did for them." "I worked there for ten years and was a top-performing employee." "We were like a family. This came out of nowhere." We want to believe the stories companies sell us, not the stats. So when we're told to pack our things in a bankers box and go home, we're shocked. *How could they do this to me? We have such a good relationship. I've contributed so much.*

While all of that may be true, and your boss and peers may see you as a person, there is someone sitting in a large, poorly decorated office with a total number of terminations they need to complete. To organizations, we are headcount. Not people. That might sound harsh, but you need to hear it.

Allow yourself to enjoy your work, build community, and have fun with the people you see forty hours a week if you can. All of that is meaningful. Your career fueling your VPL is meaningful. But it can't be the only thing filling you up. Never put the rose-colored glasses on. Understand that when your company feeds you a story about being "different" and being "the good guys," that's how they keep you hooked. Recognize that should they need to make cuts, there's no way to guarantee your protection. They are operating in the financial interest of the company at all times; the only way to protect yourself is to operate in your own interest at all times, too.

CHAPTER 2

UNTYING YOUR IDENTITY FROM WORK

So if you understand that there's no such thing as a dream job and your company might love-bomb you but will ultimately never love you, what does this mean for you? Well, babe, it means you officially have permission to untie your identity from work!

Who tied this knot in the first place?

Great news: We can blame other people for this one! Probably including your parents (sorry again, Mom). But, of course, the main culprit is companies who manipulate us into emotionally investing in them.

We spend nearly forty hours a week working, for a total of ninety thousand hours worked across the average lifetime. It's not surprising that an activity we spend so much time doing becomes a core part of our identity.

But conflating our work with our worth often starts long before we clock in to work for the first time. It starts at school.

The education system rewards "good grades" according to their (very rigid and ultimately insufficient) academic standards. Personally, if I got anything shy of an A-minus in school, I was having a literal mental breakdown. My parents stopped asking me how tests went at school because they didn't want to hear me sob over the fact that I wasn't getting A-pluses across the board. (Mom . . . sorry again.)

It's not shocking that by high school, 61 percent of teens feel immense pressure to earn good grades. Good grades mean Mom and Dad will be proud, teachers will be happy, and classmates will be impressed. They mean you'll get into a good university and have a good life. Good grades = good kid. Good grades validate our "goodness."

One day you graduate, and the desire to be told you're a good kid follows. But you were likely never taught to validate your skills, creative thinking, or talent. Instead, you spent ten-plus years of your life chasing test scores and praise.

Where does that desire for validation go after you graduate? Well, you chase validation at work. You try to get the swanky job your parents will want to brag about to their friends, get compliments from your manager, get a big shiny promotion, and more. If good grades = good kid, then good employee = good person.

You may be reading this and saying, "Emily, I don't think like this. I didn't even really care about my grades in school." To which I say: "You sure, babe?"

Getting Validation from Work

Answer yes or no to the following questions.

1. *Getting my work recognized publicly makes me feel more confident about my skills as an employee.*

2. *When I meet someone new and they ask me to tell them about myself, I often include what I do for work in my introduction.*

3. *Getting negative feedback about my work makes me feel insecure or anxious.*

4. *When I make a mistake at work, I find the feeling of nervousness or guilt can linger for hours before I truly move on.*

5. *I feel proud to share my career accolades with my loved ones.*

6. *If I were to be laid off tomorrow, it would impact my sense of identity and potentially make me question my worth.*

7. *I want the people I work with to think highly of me.*

Give yourself one point for each question you answered yes to. If you scored above a 2, you get validation from work.

For the record, almost all of us get a sense of validation from work, even if only on a subconscious level. This isn't a point of shame—it's a point of power. Once you become aware of the dopamine and validation you're chasing at work, it becomes easier to eliminate work as the source of your identity and start finding new ways to get validation that are genuinely under your control.

This isn't your fault, to be clear. We've been conditioned to identify with our jobs for centuries. Historically, many last names were tied to the jobs the individual had. These are called occupational surnames, and they were used to identify people based on the role they played in the labor market. To list just a few examples, the last name Wright was used for folks who made goods like wheels and wagons, Smith was used for blacksmiths or other metal workers, and Chamberlain was used for those who managed the chamber of wealthy people, usually in a housekeeping or guarding capacity.

Now you might be thinking, "What does this even matter? So my identity is tied to my job. What's the big deal? It sounds like everybody's is."

You're right. Everyone ties who they are to what they do. Sometimes it's extremely conscious (shout-out to that one cousin who talks about work nonstop at the family function) and other times it's not (shout-out to the people who don't care about their job until they're laid off and then have an identity crisis, wondering, "Who am I if I am not working forty hours a week?"). Honestly, though, not to sound like my mom, but if everyone jumped off a bridge, would you?

Everyone's identity is tied to work—and that's why everyone is miserable. In fact, 50 percent of employees report being stressed at work, with 19 percent of people self-reporting as feeling miserable. But even if you scroll through TikTok for five minutes, you'll see what I'm talking about. People vlogging their "midday mental breakdowns" flooded with tears and frustration as they sit quietly at their cubicles. Videos of young people spiraling and asking, "Do I really need to do this work for the next sixty years?!" Me reposting all of them. We're all unhappy with our jobs.

Having your identity tied to your job means that your happiness is largely impacted by work. Of course, intellectually, you know you're more than your job. You're able to turn off your laptop, commute home, make dinner, and watch a new show on Netflix without ruminating on the day spent in the office . . . most of the time.

But you really begin to see how tied your identity is to work when you have a bad day at the office. You made a big mistake in a presentation, you made a typo in a company-wide email, and you're starting to suspect that Bob from Accounting really doesn't like you. On those days, you close your laptop (thinking about what you could have done differently), commute home (wondering why Bob suddenly is leaving you off of emails), make dinner (feeling like such an idiot that you can't even face these people again tomorrow), and watch a new show on Netflix (hardly paying attention because you're texting your mom, asking her what she would do in this situation). Sound familiar?

It's normal for bad days to stick with us. We're human, after all. But bad days at work often make us feel like we aren't smart enough, passionate enough, detail oriented enough, or . . . good enough. So when you have a workday where you weren't on your A game or you were sucked into office drama, it impacts not only your attitudes about your work but also your sense of self overall.

Your worth is tied to your work by how you feel about your productivity, your job title, your performance feedback, and more. All of these things that are (at times) out of your control have a direct impact on how you see yourself. That's risky business.

How do most people deal with this problem? They ignore it. But all that does is put your mental and physical health at risk. Workplace stress has been shown to increase the risk of anxiety, depression, substance abuse, heart disease, ulcers, and a weakened immune system. I used to read about statistics like those and think, "This is sooo dramatic." Until I worked a job that actually made me question my sanity and I could literally feel my body shutting down. This isn't anything to play about. There are nearly 120,000 reported deaths in the US every single year that are directly tied to workplace stress.

To some extent, work will always be stressful, because, well, it's work. But the best thing you can do to prevent work from impacting your happiness and health is to set a clear boundary between your job and your sense of self.

YOUR JOB IS WHAT YOU DO, NOT WHO YOU ARE

If your self-worth is tied to your work, it's time to untie the knot before it chokes you.

Let's start by accepting that no one is immune to the worth = work trap, so stay diligent with this one.

Remember how we debunked the myth of the dream job? Let's take it a step further and replace the notion of a "dream job" with a "dream life." It sounds so much better, no?

Your Dream Life

I want you to think about your dream lifestyle. Answer the following questions in a notebook or journal.

Rank the following statements about lifestyle on a scale from 1 to 5, with 1 being not true at all and 5 being very true.

1. *Working no more than forty hours per week is important to me.*
2. *Working Monday to Friday without work on evenings or weekends is important to me.*
3. *A consistent schedule matters to me.*
4. *Requesting time off from a boss or supervisor does not bother me.*
5. *A commute of thirty minutes or less is important to me.*
6. *I am willing to travel or relocate for the right job.*
7. *It is important to me to feel like the work I do makes a difference in the world.*

Now answer the following questions about purpose.

1. *Would you rather get paid more and work a job that doesn't have a huge impact on the world, or get paid less and have a job that highly impacts the world?*

2. *Would you rather work with great people doing a job you don't love or work a job you love with people you don't enjoy?*

3. *Do you get more energy from connecting with people or working independently?*

4. *Do you feel more fulfilled by your work life or your home life?*

Next, let's get really specific about what your ideal working life looks like. In a perfect world, you'd win the lottery. But in a pretty good world, how would you answer the following questions?

1. *Your ideal self wakes up at:*

2. *Once you wake up, the first five things you do are:*

3. *How much time do you spend getting ready? What are you wearing?*

4. *What climate are you dressing for? Where do you live?*

5. *Who else is waking up in this home?*

6. *It's time for work. Where is that?*

7. *How many people do you talk to during the day? Are these people internal (like other coworkers, partners) or external (customers, vendors)?*

8. *Do you take any breaks? If so, what do those look like?*

9. *What kinds of things do you work on throughout the day that you really enjoy?*

10. *What time are you logging off?*

11. *What do you do once you get home?*

12. *How many times a week do you see friends or family?*

13. *What hobbies do you have?*

Being aware of what matters most to you will save years of your life. Being aware of your lifestyle needs can help you avoid jobs that aren't a good fit for you—or help you mentally prepare for your experience in a suboptimal job you may have to accept based on life circumstances. Information really is power. It gives you the tools to understand *why* you may be feeling miserable at work, and what small things you can change (even if it isn't the job itself) to improve overall happiness.

I see this happen all the time with my clients. They accept a job because the role itself is exactly what they're looking for, but the commute, hours, and/or interaction with coworkers isn't a great fit. But because it's the dream job, they accept it and aim to see how it goes.

It almost always goes in the same direction. Eventually, the mismatch on lifestyle catches up, and the swanky job just doesn't cut it. Often, they feel caught by surprise and didn't expect the long commute or late hours to bother them as much as it did. Doing the exercise above can help you anticipate these things so you can make more informed decisions.

YOUR LIFE OUTSIDE OF WORK

If you want to untie your worth from your work, you need to have a life outside of work that you enjoy. An existence fueled by your VPL (validation, purpose, and lifestyle). That's why meeting your lifestyle needs when you can is so important. It gives you the time and resources to invest in yourself. If your VPL goes unfulfilled in your personal life, all you have to fill the gaps with is work.

How can you achieve that? It starts with picking a job that actually gives you the lifestyle you want or creating a routine that supports your lifestyle needs as much as possible.

But above all, you need to invest in creating a life outside of work, so that your job isn't your soulmate. The best career advice in the world simply won't matter if your job ends up occupying most of your mental real estate.

Now let me pause for a quick reality check. Many times in life, you don't have the luxury to be choosy about what job you accept. Often, any job is a good job. The Dream Life exercise should be used as your North Star specifically when it makes sense to be picky. But in phases of life where being super selective isn't feasible, you can still challenge yourself to create balance in a way that honors the list of things that are important to you. For example, if you value not working weekends but there's no way around it, can you pick one day of the week for self-care, even if it's just ten minutes? If you need to commute farther than you want, can you download your favorite shows to watch on the train so the time feels more like your own?

Realistically, not every phase of life gives you the privilege to be overly picky, and many times, we have to accept a job that can pay the bills and keep the lights on. It may not be the job that offers us the perfect salary and lifestyle. But being aware of what matters to you can help you carve out small moments during the week to help you feel more alive, and it can be something you consider as you grow your career.

Wherever you're at—looking for your first role, working a job you love, or working a job you hate—the only thing that will truly free you from feeling like work is your entire life is to build a life you actually like. So let's make a game plan, step by step.

STEP 1.
GET VALIDATION FROM OTHER PLACES

What the heck happened to hobbies? A study from Harvard shows that having hobbies is directly linked to overall happiness and better well-being. Having hobbies fosters a sense of community and creativity and supports stress management. (That's what I tell myself as I watch the Real Housewives yell at each other on TV: It's healing and managing my stress.)

Of course, now, every time you have a hobby you enjoy (or are good at), everyone's first response is to tell you to make it a side hustle. Like damn, can't a girl just draw without selling it on Etsy? In this economy, who can blame your friends for suggesting ways to earn more money? But hobbies are meant to be there for fun, not for funds. The issue with Gen Zers and young millennials is that we haven't had the luxury of just having fun, because we've lived through so much economic turbulence.

Regardless, go get a hobby and watch your sense of self improve. I'm serious. Make a commitment to yourself to pick up two hobbies this year, one that's done solo and one that's group based. Maybe that's baking and yoga classes, or figure skating and trivia nights. Picking something with a set schedule that forces you to interact with others (gasp) is going to do the most good. Alternatively, if you hate people, pick a hobby where you're committing to learning a new skill. Learning new things, like a language, or cooking, or a sport, is proven to significantly increase confidence and self-perception over time.

Why this works:

- Forced mental breaks from work are game-changing. OK, so you had an awful workday. Instead of staying home and wallowing in front of the TV, you already committed to Monday night trivia. You have places to be. Answers to submit. You're forced to socialize, laugh, and build community. For a few hours, work isn't at the forefront of your mind. How refreshing. The more you do this, the more you rewire your brain to stop ruminating on work after five o'clock.

- Even if you're shit at trivia (join the club), the sense of community, collaboration, and occasional correct answers build confidence. Eventually you'll get better at whatever hobby you pick up, and studies show that improvement builds confidence. Suddenly your boss isn't the only person with the power to tell you that you've done a good job. You get to do that for yourself.

- Literally having a life outside of work will remind you that you're a human. Not a cog in a corporate machine. Life is for the living, not for the emails!

So, you're picking up an after-work hobby effective today, right?

STEP 2.
STOP LIVING FOR THE WEEKENDS

I hear you. The last thing anyone wants to do after a long-ass work-day is shower, get ready, and go out somewhere. You're tired. You've small-talked all you can small-talk. The couch sounds incredible.

But, baby, what you want and what you need are two different things.

When you give in to the post-work rot every day until Friday, you're living for the weekend—whether you realize it or not. You're putting your life on hold and saying, "I'll do that on Saturday"—and then you're shocked when your weekends are so jam-packed with cleaning, grocery shopping, self-care, and socializing that you can't fit it all in. Living like this puts so much pressure on those precious two days. I often hear my clients refer to "weekend me" and "work-week me," as if they're two separate people, and although that's a very common coping mechanism to deal with the fact that we only have two days off every week, it usually does more harm than good. Instead of making sure we have moments of joy throughout the week, we're waiting to feel alive on the weekend. That isn't any way to live.

So if you want to untie your identity from work, you need to have an identity to replace it with from Monday to Friday. Activity time! Make a list of five things you genuinely look forward to on the weekends. For example, I love doing the following on weekends:

- Grocery shopping at local farmers markets (I'm obsessed with this)
- Grabbing dinner at new spots with my girlfriends
- Morning hot yoga classes
- Visiting my parents for the weekend in my hometown
- Getting my nails done while sipping a big coffee

Yet, realistically, here's what I would do after work by default:

- Come home
- Prepare dinner
- Watch *The Real Housewives*
- Wallow

There's a bit of a mismatch, no?

Now, from your list of five, pick at least two you can incorporate throughout the week. For me, it would look like this:

- *Grocery shopping at local farmers markets:* The markets aren't open on weekdays, so this is a no.

- *Grabbing dinner at new spots with my girlfriends:* Doable if I pick a spot close to the office and meet friends there right after work.

- *Morning hot yoga classes:* I'm not waking up at 5 a.m.! What am I, a fitness influencer?

- *Visiting my parents for the weekend in my hometown:* This is off the table, as my parents live an hour away.

- *Getting my nails done while sipping a big coffee:* Also doable after work if I make the coffee decaf.

Great news! You've now identified two things that make you feel like *you* that you can do during the week. Your homework now is to push through the "I don't feel like it" of it all and make plans to invest in what brings you joy. Remember, your job doesn't need to be the love of your life. It can simply fund a lifestyle you love.

Your workweek now might look something like:

- Monday: Rot at home (everyone hates Mondays)
- Tuesday: Group hobby or solo hobby night
- Wednesday: Stay in
- Thursday: Dinner or a movie with friends
- Friday: Freedom

I can't even tell you how many of my clients have started to incorporate things they love about their weekends into their workweek. It sounds so small and so commonsense, but it's incredibly easy to get wrapped up in our working world and forget that we deserve to invest in the things that make us feel alive.

By the way, as a friendly reminder, social activities with your coworkers don't count (unless they truly are your friends). But we'll talk about your coworkers later.

STEP 3. FIND BEAUTY IN THE MUNDANE

Step three to feeling like you have a sense of identity that doesn't only come from work is to find beauty in the mundane. Repeat this to yourself: *I'm a person, not an employee.* IAPNAE. (Unhinged acronym, but it'll get the job done.) Find little IAPNAE moments throughout your day. They give you a chance to break the tether to work and remind yourself it isn't that serious.

Remember, your company will probably try to gaslight you into thinking everything you do is critical, everything is life and death. Having IAPNAE moments reminds you that you're truly floating on a rock in space and that money is made up. It's an opportunity to be grounded in the reality that you are a whole and complete person. This is especially great if you're in a job you hate or that doesn't meet your lifestyle needs.

The best IAPNAE hacks I know:

- Reclaim your commute. Obviously all of us hate commuting, and we all agree we should be getting paid for the time it takes to get to the office, right? But what if we intentionally picked an activity that brought us some degree of joy so that the time spent on the train or in the car felt like *ours*? Read a book, play Nintendo Switch, or listen to a podcast or audiobook you love. What small thing can you do to make your commute feel less painful?

- Bust out your nice stuff—your fancy hand creams, luxurious lip mask, maybe even flavored coffee syrups. Leave it at your desk, whether you work in-office or at home. Anything to incorporate some degree of luxury into your day so you get to feel like at least one element of your morning is centered on self-care.

- Get dressed in clothes you genuinely enjoy. After all, 96 percent of people say how they feel changes based on what they're wearing. Put on clothes that make you feel like you.

- Take IAPNAE breaks. These go beyond just your lunch break. These are breaks you take with the specific intention of feeling like a human. Take at least one break a day to do something that you would do on the weekend, like a quick online shopping browse or calling your best friend for ten minutes. Something that grounds you by saying, "Hey, you're a full person outside of this job. You know that, right?"

- Recite IAPNAE affirmations. In moments of stress at work, I recommend repeating comforting phrases like:
    - If I died today, they would have my job posted by Tuesday. I am ultimately very replaceable.
    - I don't get paid enough to be this stressed. Let me take a breath.
    - I won't look back on my life and wish that I worked more.
    - If they wanted me to stress about my job on the weekends, they would pay me for it.

STEP 4.
WATCH YOUR MOUTH

Pay attention to the way you talk to yourself. We'll go deeper into impostor syndrome and how to stop being so hard on yourself later on, but for now, I'll say: If you expect to have a healthy relationship to work but you're an avid negative self-talker, I got some bad news for you. Your negative self-talk is going to damage your career and your life. It's as simple as that.

How we think and speak to ourselves undoubtedly impacts how we see the world around us, and how we see ourselves. The National Science Foundation reports that the average person has just over six thousand thoughts every day (only 10 percent of that if you're one of my ex-boyfriends). Of those thoughts, 80 percent are negative, and 95 percent are the exact same repetitive thoughts as the day before—and (spoiler) those are also about 80 percent negative.

Negative self-talk is directly related to worse mental and physical health, decreased productivity, challenges with interpersonal relationships, reduced performance at work, and way more.

When it comes to work, negative self-talk usually pops up in the following ways:

- Catastrophizing: Every problem is automatically the worst-case scenario.
- Personalization: Everything, and I mean *everything*, is personal.
- Procrastination: Everything will get done later, because you don't have faith in yourself right now.
- Perfectionism: Nothing is ever good enough, because nothing is ever perfect.

- Polarization: Things are good or bad, black or white. There is no nuance.

Constantly telling yourself that you're an idiot, or that every mistake you make is the biggest deal in the world, will actually reshape your brain—and not in a cute shapewear way. Your brain naturally adapts to your needs by creating neural pathways to help you repeat familiar behaviors and thoughts.

The more you practice drawing or speaking French, the better you become at it. By the same token, when you think negative things about yourself, your brain develops familiar pathways to encourage this, and it becomes your default mode of thought. If you're always thinking critical thoughts about your life and career, your brain will literally create neural pathways to reinforce this process. The more you think these thoughts, the more deeply this pathway is reinforced.

> "I made a mistake at work." → "I'm a stupid idiot." → "I'll keep making these mistakes forever."

The good news is that the same habits used to create these pathways can be leveraged to create different pathways. So instead of training yourself to think you're the biggest idiot at work, or that you're awful at your job, what if you trained yourself to operate with a bit more balance?

> "I made a mistake at work." → "It's just work, everyone makes mistakes, and every problem has a solution." → "I'll handle the mistake, and it'll be OK."

To return to the examples of work-related negative self-talk above, you could make changes like these:

OLD (UNHELPFUL) THOUGHT	NEW THOUGHT
"I made this mistake at work. Now I'm going to get fired."	"I made a mistake, and realistically everything is going to be OK. Even if it isn't, I will be OK."
"I didn't get the promotion. My boss must hate me and want me to fail."	"The reason I didn't get the promotion is not that I'm not good enough as a person. I'll ask my boss for feedback so I understand where to improve."
"The second I start this, I'm going to mess it up, so I don't even want to look at it."	"Done but imperfect is better than not done at all. I'll start and ask for help if I need it."
"Yeah, most of the presentation went well, but I skipped that one slide, so it was all a failure."	"It wasn't perfect, but neither are the people around me, and they're doing just fine."
"I'm the best employee ever." Five minutes later: "I'm the worst employee on this team."	"Nothing is black-and-white. No one else on my team is 100 percent right or 100 percent wrong, so why would I be?"

What if, for one week, you stopped using language that made work personal and then kept track of how you felt about yourself overall? I think I know the answer.

It's also not a bad idea to stop immediately asking people what they do for work when we first meet them. Or jumping into "How is work?" when we catch up with friends and family. When you're intentional about focusing on nonprofessional wins and life changes with the people around you, you'll be amazed at how much you start remembering that you, too, are a person outside of work. And your job can only stress you out so much when it's not your everything. (That's why I also recommend having multiple boyfriends. Kidding.)

STEP 5. BOUNDARIES, BABY

Boundaries feels like the buzzword of the century. In fact, it's gotten so buzzy that sometimes people take the concept to unnecessary extremes. Your mom sneezed too loud and it disturbed your peace? Set a boundary. That person texted you four minutes later than they said they would? Block them. It's a boundary.

Setting boundaries isn't supposed to be an excuse to be an asshole. It's supposed to be a way to set rules to stop assholes from taking advantage of you. For example, a healthy boundary might be "If you keep swearing at me, I'm going to end the conversation and leave the room." Or "If my boss emails me after five p.m., I will not respond until the next day during work hours." The final step to untying your worth from your work is setting boundaries that honor the fact that you're a whole-ass person outside of your cubicle.

All the work you did in steps 1 through 4 will be for nothing if you can't set boundaries around work, so really this step is the most important. And boundaries only work when you're willing to enforce them. This commitment first starts with yourself. Do you respect your needs enough to protect them from people who don't respect them?

For each boundary you set, clearly define what the consequence will be should someone step over it. A consequence can be as simple as not responding until Monday if you get an email on the weekend. It could also mean cc'ing your manager on all emails with that one coworker who constantly throws you under the bus. Boundaries deserve more real estate, so we're going to crack into this in chapter 11.

BRINGING IT ALL TOGETHER

Regardless of where you're at in your career, whether you're looking for a new job or deep into your professional journey, you will *never* feel like you're satisfied or mentally sound until you untie your self-worth from your job. Let's review the five steps to make that happen.

STEP	WHY IT WORKS	YOUR HOMEWORK
Get validation outside of work.	When work inevitably knocks your confidence, you'll have other sources of confidence to make you feel worthy.	Go get a hobby, dude.
Stop living for the weekends.	Your job will feel like your whole world if you have nothing else going on between Monday and Friday.	Incorporate two activities into your workweek that you usually reserve for the weekends.
Find beauty in the mundane.	Grounding yourself in small IAPNAE moments reminds you that you're a person, not an employee.	Pick at least one IAPNAE moment you will bake into your workweek.
Watch your mouth.	Stopping the cycle of negative self-talk will save you from feeling deeply insecure and miserable.	Every time you think or say something negative about yourself, swap it out for something neutral or positive.

STEP	WHY IT WORKS	YOUR HOMEWORK
Boundaries, baby.	When you honor your time and emotional boundaries, you put yourself, and not your job, first.	Make a list of boundaries around your time and relationships at work. Write out what you'll do when your boundary is crossed so you can hold yourself accountable.

This chapter really boils down to you finding things other than work to satisfy your VPL, so that your job doesn't define you. Your job will never love you back, so stop trying to love your job and start trying to love your life.

CHAPTER 3

THE HUNT

So now you're aware of the fact that your job is never going to love you back. There is so much power in awareness. For example, pay attention to your posture right now. When you read that sentence, did you adjust your posture to be a little more upright and straight? Most people do. You didn't need specific instructions to do so. Once you were aware that you were hunched over with a kink in your neck, you adjusted.

Your career is a lot like your bad posture. Once you become aware of the ways your employers will take advantage of you and how your natural inclination will be to wrap your identity in your career, the less likely you are to let it happen. Trust me, you'll be happier for it. (But for real, sit up straight, too.)

Now that we've built the awareness to make sure you won't lose your mind in your job, it's time to get to the practical part. Because while your job isn't going to love you back, Momma's still gotta pay the bills. This chapter is going to break down exactly how to navigate the modern job search without losing your mind or your confidence. I'm going to cover how the job search actually works from a recruiter's perspective so you can hack the system.

Everything I'm about to share is stuff that I've picked up in my career and have used directly with my clients. This information is never, *ever* going out of style. Sure, the platforms and interview methods may evolve over time, but this chapter is full of fundamental job-hunting skills that will be relevant forever.

But first, a reality check: Remember how I don't want you to mentally spiral or tie your worth to your career? That applies to your job search, too. So let's just ground ourselves with some facts for a moment. In my experience, I've found that:

1. The average job search takes between five to eight months in North America, depending on the industry.

2. A significant portion of jobs that are filled are never even posted.

3. Up to 80 percent of jobs are filled by referrals and word of mouth.

So if it feels like your job search is taking forever, you aren't alone. In our modern working world, the process is drawn out, network intensive, and frankly, kind of bullshit. That's why you need to promise me that you're not going to internalize the mess that is the job search, because, truthfully, it has nothing to do with you. I'm telling you as a careers expert: It's job hunting that sucks. Not you.

We'll get into how to avoid job search burnout in more detail later, but for now, please refer to these affirmations to avoid being hard on yourself during this process.

Job Hunt Affirmations

I used to think positive affirmations were silly, but from one skeptic to another: Try them. And literally say them out loud—it's neuroscience. Repeat after me:

- Not having a job offer doesn't mean that I am not a qualified and strong candidate. My skills are strong, and the right opportunity is coming.
- Getting rejected from opportunities doesn't mean I wasn't good enough.
- The fact that this process is discouraging isn't a reflection of me as a person or of my abilities.
- I am a deeply intelligent and worthy person, regardless of where I am in my career.
- I am a whole, empathetic, fun, and important person outside of work.
- My career and being financially stable is important, and I will succeed in both.
- I am literally floating on a rock looking for a job that was made up by some guy a hundred years ago. None of this matters.

You've defined the jobs that seem like a good fit, and you determined the validation, purpose, and lifestyle (VPL) factors that you're taking into account when conducting this search. It's time to put it into action.

TIMING IS EVERYTHING

When is the best time to apply for jobs? Whenever you realize you need a job. I know this might sound like a hot take when there are so many people online telling you to wait until "busy recruitment seasons" to give your application a better chance at standing out. But think about it: If everyone is doing that, no one is standing out.

Sure, January tends to be a busy season for hiring, as companies have their annual budgets reset in the new year. But waiting until busy season isn't the right call if there are jobs posted today that you're interested in. Don't use seasonality as an excuse to procrastinate. Thinking about getting things done isn't the same as getting things done.

I would also argue that *when* you apply matters much less than *what you do after* you apply . . . but let me not get ahead of myself. Understanding that the average job search can take months, think about your ideal start date for a new gig, and start applying for jobs at least five months before that date. This is true at any level in your career, whether you're an intern, a new graduate, or a CEO. So, the second you want a new job, start applying for one. Don't listen to anyone telling you different.

MYTH:
Wait until peak recruitment seasons to apply for jobs.

REALITY:
When you see a job you like, apply for it.

LOOKING BEHIND THE HIRING CURTAIN

When I first started working as a recruiter, I was shocked by how little I'd actually understood about the recruitment process. If there's one thing that became abundantly clear to me, it's that the candidates who understood the system were better able to hack it.

And those candidates were very often the friend/child/cousin of a very senior person at the company. Great news: You're now my friend/child/cousin, and it's time for me to give you a peek behind the hiring curtain.

THE PLAYERS

There are really two core players you'll be dealing with in the job search: the hiring manager and the recruiter.

1. The Hiring Manager: This is usually the person who would be your boss if you get the job—the final boss, if you will. The hiring manager determines the job responsibilities, makes the hiring decision, and sets the salary and start date. This is the person calling the shots.

2. The Recruiter: Think of the recruiter as a spokesperson for the hiring manager. Recruiters can work either in-house at the company you're interviewing with or at an agency hired by the company to fill a position. In both cases, recruiters don't call the final shots, but they heavily influence the manager and are the ultimate gatekeeper between you and the manager. The recruiter's goal is usually to advocate both for your interests and the interests of the company. Having a recruiter on your side will make your job search a million times easier.

THE PROCESS

Have you ever wondered what's happening internally at a company when they post a job? I'm here to demystify the process for you.

1. **The role gets approved.** At every company, in order for a job to be posted, it needs to be approved by either finance, HR, or some combination of the two, to ensure there's a budget for the salary and approval on the title—in other words, to make sure there's enough money to pay the person they hire. This means almost every job has a salary band determined by the time it's posted, otherwise it wouldn't have been approved.

   > Tip: *If a recruiter tries to play the "I don't know the budget" card, don't accept that as an excuse for them not being transparent about compensation expectations. Even if they don't know the specific numbers, they usually have a general sense of budget.*

2. **The job description is written.** The hiring manager writes a list of things the applicant needs to be able to do—or at least what they *hope* the applicant will be able to do. When I tell you not to take job descriptions too seriously, I mean it. Eighty percent of the time, a job description is written like a wish list of everything the ideal candidate should have, and most managers understand that their wish list isn't completely realistic.

   > Tip: *If you see a job you aren't 100 percent qualified for, apply anyway.*

3. **The job is posted.** The company posts the job description online. As a college student applying for internships, I believed the advice I heard online to only use certain job boards or to not use LinkedIn to apply for jobs. Now that I've worked in HR, I can confirm that

is *false*. Most companies use an applicant tracking system (ATS), an internal platform for posting jobs, receiving applications, booking interviews, etc. The company posts the job once, directly from their ATS, and it funnels out to all the job websites. Likewise, applications from all those websites funnel in through the ATS.

> Tip: *Your application is going to the same place no matter which site you use, so use the site that is easiest for you and don't waste your time stressing.*

4. Applicants are reviewed. I was told by my college classmates that the best time to apply for jobs is Sunday night so that your résumé will be at the top of the pile when recruiters start reviewing applications on Monday morning. But once again, after working on teams of incredible recruiters, I quickly learned that the rumor mill was wrong. The Sunday night theory may be true for some recruiters, but certainly not for all, and therefore it isn't a reliable variable to factor into your job search. Some recruiters check applications every morning, every evening, every other day, or (spoiler alert) never.

> Tip: *There's no way to predict when recruiters are reviewing applications, and in many cases, shitty recruiters never review them at all. Just apply for jobs when you have time.*

5. Recruiters prescreen candidates. After reviewing applications, the recruiter develops a short list of candidates who they think match the qualifications. Then they book a prescreen call to suss out initial fit.

This chat usually lets the recruiter review your overall experience and whether you're a fit for the company and the role before they present your résumé to the hiring manager. There may be as few as five or as many as a hundred candidates in this stage of the process competing against you.

> Tip: *Don't worry about the number of candidates you're going up against. It won't matter if you're the one.*

6. Interviews are conducted. After the recruiter determines that you might be a fit for the position, they'll present a group of candidates to the manager for review. The manager, based on the résumé and prescreen notes, will choose who is moving forward in the process.

   > Tip: *Start preparing your introduction for the beginning of the interview. (You'll learn how to ace an interview in detail on page 109.)*

7. Offers are made. After your interviews, the team will determine who is the best fit for the position and move forward with an offer for one, while keeping the runner-up candidate on the hook.

   > Tip: *Just because you have a job offer doesn't mean you need to accept it. You need to make sure the offer in front of you satisfies your VPL. (We'll get into how to evaluate and negotiate an offer in chapter 9.)*

Now that you have a grasp of the overall hiring process at a company, let's go into more detail.

THE CORPORATE CHECKOUT

As mentioned in step 3 of the hiring process, most companies use an internal software called an applicant tracking system (ATS) to post jobs, receive applications, and so on. The ATS is an internal system used to collect every single application, store candidate data, and create offer letters. Think of it as a one-stop shop for recruiters. Although the ATS is a helpful tool that every single recruiter uses, the system itself isn't as smart as you might think it is. The ATS isn't the sole reviewer of your application, and it isn't throwing your résumé out if you don't meet specific keywords. What it's doing is ranking candidates it "thinks" may be a good fit for the role, based on keywords, location, and years of experience.

There is a common misconception that the ATS will throw out résumés that don't match keywords found in the job description, or that it will dispose of candidates based on unreadable résumés. And although having an easily digestible résumé is important, it isn't because the ATS is some über-smart robot that holds the future of your career in its shiny metal hand. The ATS can help rank and prioritize candidates and, in some cases, even leverage AI to predict which candidates are the best fit, but although the system is very helpful, it isn't able to do a recruiter's job all by itself (at least not today). Recruiters use the ATS as a tool to help filter and rank candidates in the system, but they usually aren't using the ATS to screen candidates without a human review. When we see more advancement in AI capabilities, this will likely evolve, but for now, most organizations see recruiter review as king.

In fact, we're already starting to see discrimination lawsuits pop up around the topic of AI-powered ATSes systemically disadvantaging underrepresented groups. Even though some systems can use AI to filter candidates, most organizations understand the limitations of this and are operating with caution. Instead of exclusively having AI review your résumé, most recruiters manually read every single résumé they come across, even at the big sexy tech companies.

How do I know? Well, I did it. The ATS may be able to filter your résumé to the top of the pile if it thinks you are a match, but either way, a recruiter usually reviews your profile manually. So it truly is a tool that a *real human recruiter* uses to review applications; it isn't as advanced as we think.

With thousands of applications for every single job, how does a recruiter get through them all? On average, a recruiter looks at your résumé for six seconds before determining whether or not they'll move forward with you as a candidate. Only six seconds. How are they reading everything you wrote in that short a time? I have big news: They're not. Baby, they're not reading your résumé at all.

The average recruiter is *skimming*, not *reading*, your résumé. Those are two very different things. *Skimming* a textbook before an exam will give you a high-level sense of the subject matter, some key words, and maybe a notable quote or two. *Reading* the textbook means you genuinely understand the material inside and out.

Recruiters for the most part aren't trying to understand every element of you inside and out. They're just trying to determine if you might be a fit, quickly. The fate of your candidacy may not rest in the hands of a robot, but it does rest in a six-second-long skim from a recruiter. (Truly, I don't know which I prefer.)

You only have six precious seconds to sell the recruiter on your experience well enough to move you forward for a prescreening interview. How do recruiters do this?

They give you what I like to call the corporate checkout. Basically, this means they give your résumé a brief once-over, starting at the top and skimming their way down, with their eyes going to a few core spots. Which is why it's so important for your résumé to make a good impression, regardless of the finer details.

As the recruiter checks you out, the conclusions they're drawing about your candidacy aren't necessarily the accurate ones—they're the easy ones. For example, the human brain is naturally going to assume that whatever is at the top of the page or whatever it reads first is the most important. If your résumé leads with your school experience, the recruiter will subconsciously assume that you're early in your career. If your résumé leads with work experience, the recruiter will subconsciously assume you're further along in your career.

This is why if you're a new graduate, your résumé should be one page, maximum. Remember, you only have six seconds, so why would you risk information getting lost over two pages when it could be put into one? And you don't necessarily need a "professional summary" section, given your experience level (but if you opt for one, I'll give you a script later in this chapter).

If you have two or more years of experience, still aim for a one-page résumé. It's not the end of the world if you have two pages, but my warning is still true: The more pages you have, the higher the risk that content gets ignored during the six-second checkout.

DISCRIMINATION

No matter where you're at in your career, never, *ever* include these on your résumé:

- Photos of you
- Markers of your age
- Markers of religion
- Criminal history

Why? Discrimination is alive and well, and even when recruiters think they're being completely fair-minded, they may subconsciously discriminate while making snap judgments during that six-second checkout. We can't talk about the job search without acknowledging that.

I often have people ask me why they can't include a photo of themselves on their résumé. After all, it's a great way to put a face to a name and add a bit of personality. The reality is that adding pictures of yourself to your résumé opens you up to a world of bias and discrimination. I understand how this may be confusing, because it's incredibly important to have a photo on your LinkedIn profile—but that's because it's the norm on that particular platform. The risk of not having a photo on LinkedIn is higher than the risk of having one. For your résumé, it's the opposite. On LinkedIn, a headshot helps prove you're not a bot or a scammer. On your résumé, it opens up opportunities for discrimination based on gender, race, religion, age, and more (at least in North America, where headshots on résumés are uncommon).

But, Emily, it's 2026; is hiring discrimination even legal? Just because we've made progress on an issue doesn't mean the issue is solved. In fact, a recent study found that very little progress has actually been made in terms of hiring discrimination since the 1990s. The researchers assessed ninety studies of 174,000 job applications from Canada, France, Germany, Great Britain, the Netherlands, and the United States. The goal was to determine whether protected groups like Black, Middle Eastern or North African, Latin or Hispanic, and Asian communities saw a decline in racism in the hiring process. Even with several antidiscrimination laws being passed in recent history, the researchers reported that "the biggest takeaway was that on average, there has been no change in hiring discrimination when aggregating all six countries together." France was the only country that showed a significant reduction in discrimination. Most other countries held steady over time, with some even trending upward.

Unsurprisingly, applicants of color from all backgrounds in the study needed to send in 50 percent more applications per interview callback on average. Now, most of these folks were not putting photos of themselves on their résumés, but key markers like names and LinkedIn profiles were taken into account. I'd bet this data would be even more damning if attaching a headshot to your application was the norm.

Maybe you've heard of the famous 2004 study that determined that applicants with "white-sounding" names got 50 percent more callbacks from employers than those whose names sounded Black. This study was re-created in 2024 and found that employers, based on the names on résumés, called back white-sounding candidates as much as 24 percent more than Black-sounding candidates. Is this a slight improvement? Yes. But after years of "progress," this data tells us a clear message: Discrimination is still alive and well in the recruitment process.

Discrimination can take many forms. Sometimes it's very obvious, like in that one episode of *That's So Raven* (probably the best show of all time, I'm sure we'd all agree). The show's psychic teen protagonist, Raven, is interviewing for a retail job at a clothing store, and as an incredibly stylish and outgoing girl who even designs her own clothes, she's the perfect candidate. After acing the interview, she's shocked to find out she didn't get the job—until she has a psychic vision of the store manager telling someone that she "doesn't hire Black people."

This type of *overt* racism can and does contribute to disparities in the hiring process or at work. But just as often, the discrimination in corporate America is more subtle. It's hidden from plain sight, which makes it harder to detect, call out, and deal with. This is called *covert* racism, and it shows up in everything from the academic system to the job search process to promotions and beyond. Gender, age, and other intersections of identity also factor into this, but data shows that race tends to be the largest driver of hiring-based inequity.

This also plays into the wage gap and pay inequity. I often hear people use the term *wage gap* to describe the difference in earnings between men and women, but that's missing a big part of the story. The truth is, white women tend to earn about 83 cents for every dollar a white man makes, whereas Black men only make 71 cents on the dollar and Black women tend to earn just 63 cents per dollar. The factors that contribute to this gap are overt, covert, and systemic. So when we talk about the importance of hiring and promoting top talent, this also means paying and promoting people fairly.

Something that doesn't get enough mainstream media attention is the promotion gap as it relates to discrimination. In addition to discrimination in the hiring process, this is also seen as folks grow at the company. For example, Black employees make up 12 percent of entry-level workers and only 7 percent of managerial roles. This is not from a lack of desire or skill; this is a direct result of structural inequity. There is a lack of recognition, advocacy, and support. This is one of the many reasons salary and promotion rate transparency is so important: Organizations need to be held accountable. In many states, we are starting to see mandated salary transparency on job postings and online, which is a start. But there is so much more that needs to be done to bridge this gap.

All of this to say, the system is broken, and the biases that people may hold are outside of your control. What you can control is what companies you're willing to work for, based on your experience, and the grace you extend yourself when you run up against barriers you didn't ask for in the hiring process. If you're like me, cisgender and white, you can also recognize the privilege and power you hold. One day, you may be a recruiter, hiring manager, or team leader, so you need to start checking your biases before they cause serious harm.

And the final thing you can control: no photos on your résumé. Just to try and protect yourself from any additional layers of discrimination.

WHAT JOBS SHOULD YOU BE APPLYING FOR?

You can have the best application in the world and be as mentally prepared as you can be, but if you're not applying to the right jobs, you're wasting your time. Having a clear understanding of what jobs you're targeting is mission critical! Otherwise, you're going to end up wasting so much time and energy applying and getting really crummy results.

If you're new to the corporate world or looking to change career paths, the Your Hit List exercise in chapter 1 should give you a good idea of the types of jobs that are a good fit for you. If you're happy in your career path but are looking for the next jump, consider roles that are the same title/level or one or two levels above. If you're stuck on the job titles that work best for your level of experience, reference this table:

1–4 YEARS OF EXPERIENCE	4–10 YEARS OF EXPERIENCE	10+ YEARS OF EXPERIENCE
Coordinator	Intermediate ______	Principal
Analyst	Senior ______	Senior manager
Junior ______	Manager ______	Head of ______
______Level 1	Team lead ______	
	Lead ______	

But let's not get *too* attached to these titles, because all job descriptions are kind of made up and bullshit.

When I first moved into a senior recruiter role, the job description asked for a long list of experience that, frankly, I didn't have, including more years of experience than I was bringing to the table. Had I listened to the suggested requirements on the job posting and *not* applied, I wouldn't have been connected to the job that doubled my salary and changed the course of my career. Interestingly, women tend to only apply for jobs when they meet close to 100 percent of the requirements, while men tend to apply for jobs where they meet roughly 60 percent.

This is a sign to stop taking yourself out of the race. Don't be your own biggest hater! Let *them* tell you that you aren't qualified. The worst-case scenario is you don't hear back and nothing changes.

If you meet 60 percent of the qualifications, apply for the damn job!

Reality Check: Fake Job Postings

I do want you to be wary of the rising number of fake job postings. Especially in this era of sneaky layoffs, many companies post job postings that literally are not real. They have no intention of hiring anyone; they just want to make it look like their company is hiring or mask negative press from recent layoffs. If you notice a job posting has been live for eight months or more, or that it has been posted and reposted over and over, that may be a sign it's fake. It's completely safe to apply for these roles, but if you don't hear back, that doesn't reflect badly on you. The job you applied for may not even exist. It's also important to be mindful of phishing scams disguised as job opportunities. Red flags for these include spammy or vague texts and interviews that ask you to pay a fee or provide social media login information.

BRINGING IT ALL TOGETHER

Your peek behind the recruitment curtain is now over. You should have a pretty solid understanding of the recruitment process, what systems you need to be aware of, and most importantly, the permission not to take this shit personally. Job hunting sucks. They don't call it job shopping—it's a vicious, labor-intensive hunt! And now that you know what you're getting into, let's get your application ready.

CHAPTER 4

APPLY YOURSELF

Now that you know who will be reading your job application and how they'll be evaluating it, it's time to get into the nitty-gritty of that application. Don't you dare start applying for jobs without reading this chapter. I'm serious. I'll be mad at you. Because your job application is a direct reflection of your personal brand that can stick with you long beyond the timeframe of this specific job you've applied to.

When a recruiter starts the search for a candidate, one of the places they may look is in the ATS (remember, that's the applicant tracking system) to search through previous applicants. And boom, there you are. But if you didn't give your résumé the attention it needed on the first job you applied for, it'll get passed over again. You could be getting rejected from jobs that you didn't even know you were being considered for because your application wasn't the best it could be.

Plus, if there's one thing I've learned about working in recruiting, it's that recruiters *talk*. It's our job. Recruiters are paid to speak all day long. And in a job where you're constantly evaluating talent (and often dealing with pretty difficult people), recruiters talk *about their candidates*.

"Evan, did you see this résumé for the software manager role? I just came across it in the ATS. I think it would be good. Want me to forward it?"

"Sandra, I was thinking of this candidate for the marketing role, but I'm on the fence. Can I get your eyes on this?"

Recruitment is more art than science, so naturally, recruiters lean on each other for perspective. The perspective may be about an incredible profile that the team is going to keep an eye on, or a candidate profile that is not a good fit. No matter the city you live in, I promise you that the recruiter community is smaller than you think. There are candidates who gave me an experience so hellish that I will never hire them for the rest of my career, and there are candidates who took rejection with so much grace that I would hire them on the spot for the next role I have. Your reputation outlives the role you apply for.

The good news is that your résumé doesn't need to be groundbreaking, earth-shattering, or iconic in order to be good. The goal is not to have a perfect résumé, it's to have a résumé that simply isn't bad. If your résumé isn't bad, then you're good.

YOUR RÉSUMÉ DESERVES A MAKEOVER

I've coached thousands of people one-on-one on the makings of an incredible résumé, and I firmly believe it boils down to three core elements: design, data, and details. (Hey, if DDD is good enough for Dolly Parton, it's good enough for me.) Let's take a closer look at each element.

DESIGN

Remember, most recruiters are only giving your résumé a six-second corporate checkout. Good design is imperative, because you can't afford to have the recruiter waste any precious seconds trying to navigate your résumé. I know I sound like Steve Jobs launching the iPod, but it really does need to be intuitive, easy, and timeless.

In this wildly competitive labor market, many people think that designing a visually interesting résumé will help you stand out against other candidates. Those people are wrong. The challenge today is less about having a state-of-the-art résumé and more about actually getting your résumé opened by a recruiter. The post-pandemic job market has nearly tripled the average number of applications each position receives. From a labor-market perspective, we have more candidates than jobs available, and that gap isn't likely to close in the near future. So a quirky résumé, although it may be a great conversation starter, isn't the secret sauce to getting noticed by recruiters. A quickly digestible résumé is.

The year could be 2010 or 2070, and all of this will be true. A timeless, simple résumé will almost always get you further ahead. And as technology evolves to automate more of the recruitment process, the need for a simple and data-forward résumé will only be stronger.

The design of your résumé is responsible for the first impression your profile makes on a recruiter. That's why you don't want any funky fonts, funky flows, funky colors, or funky visuals. Save the funky for the sharp cheeses in your fridge. The problem isn't that recruiters lack the creative vision to appreciate bold colors and unusual fonts; the problem is that these things soak up precious milliseconds in the recruiter's subconscious mind, ultimately taking away from the important content you want the recruiter to be reviewing.

The ideal résumé format varies slightly, based on your industry and level of experience, but should err on the side of strategically basic. Here's what I would recommend.

Notice there are no flashy visuals. Everything is simple, with default colors, fonts, and formatting.

You have permission to be cautiously creative with design for newer-school industries like marketing, design, and software

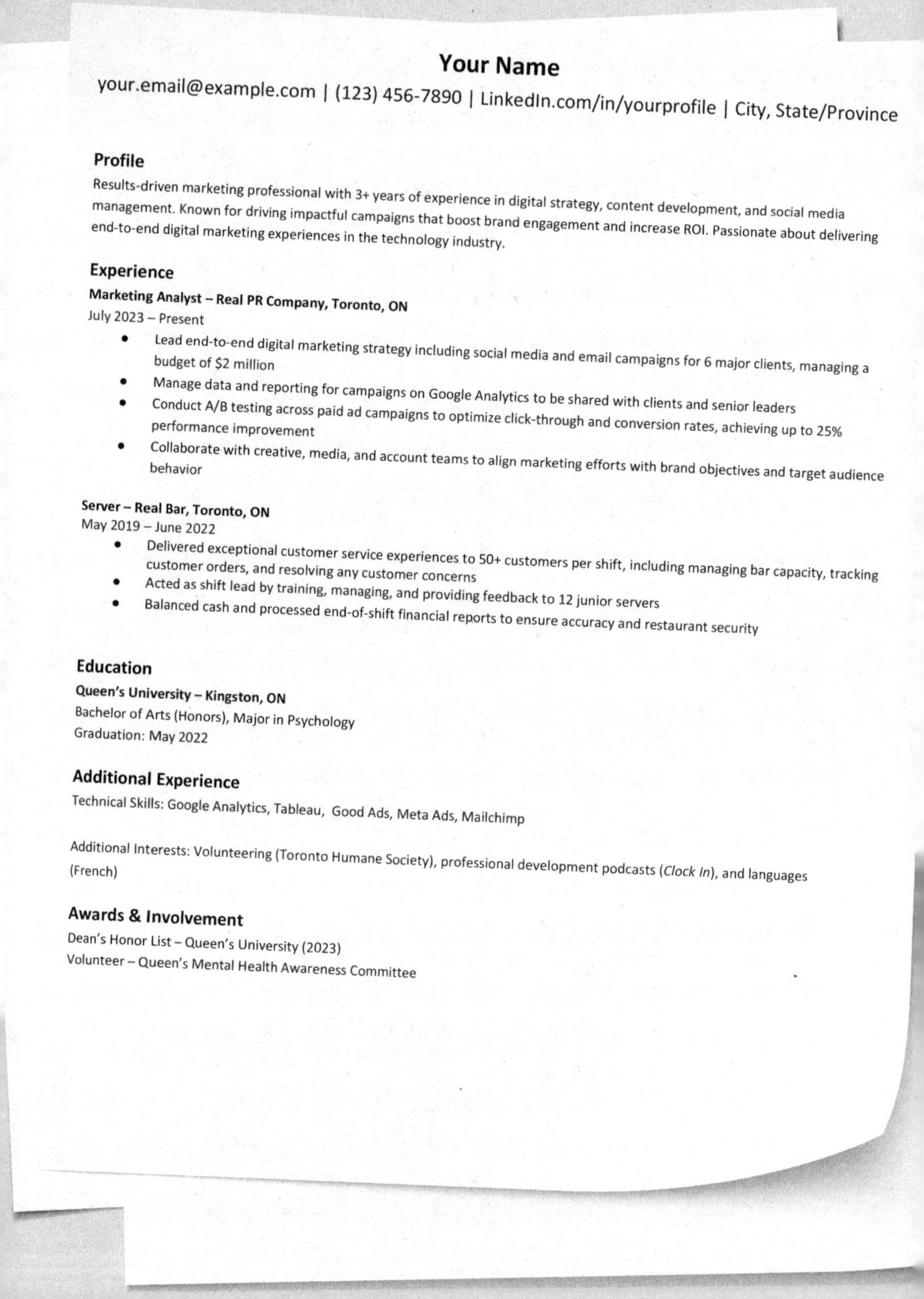

Your Name

your.email@example.com | (123) 456-7890 | LinkedIn.com/in/yourprofile | City, State/Province

Profile

Results-driven marketing professional with 3+ years of experience in digital strategy, content development, and social media management. Known for driving impactful campaigns that boost brand engagement and increase ROI. Passionate about delivering end-to-end digital marketing experiences in the technology industry.

Experience

Marketing Analyst – Real PR Company, Toronto, ON
July 2023 – Present

- Lead end-to-end digital marketing strategy including social media and email campaigns for 6 major clients, managing a budget of $2 million
- Manage data and reporting for campaigns on Google Analytics to be shared with clients and senior leaders
- Conduct A/B testing across paid ad campaigns to optimize click-through and conversion rates, achieving up to 25% performance improvement
- Collaborate with creative, media, and account teams to align marketing efforts with brand objectives and target audience behavior

Server – Real Bar, Toronto, ON
May 2019 – June 2022

- Delivered exceptional customer service experiences to 50+ customers per shift, including managing bar capacity, tracking customer orders, and resolving any customer concerns
- Acted as shift lead by training, managing, and providing feedback to 12 junior servers
- Balanced cash and processed end-of-shift financial reports to ensure accuracy and restaurant security

Education

Queen's University – Kingston, ON
Bachelor of Arts (Honors), Major in Psychology
Graduation: May 2022

Additional Experience

Technical Skills: Google Analytics, Tableau, Good Ads, Meta Ads, Mailchimp

Additional Interests: Volunteering (Toronto Humane Society), professional development podcasts (*Clock In*), and languages (French)

Awards & Involvement

Dean's Honor List – Queen's University (2023)
Volunteer – Queen's Mental Health Awareness Committee

engineering, but when in doubt, use a traditional format. If you're not sure if your job counts as old-school or new-school, take this little quiz:

1. Is your industry something that existed sixty years ago?

2. Is your industry something that your grandparents fundamentally understand exists?

3. Do you need to wear formal workwear to the office?

If you answered yes to two or more of those questions, you work in an old-school job, and if you answered no, you're new-school. One type of work is not better than the other; they just require slightly different tricks to hack the job search process and the career ladder overall.

When it comes time to actually select your résumé's design, please don't go buying a template online! I don't hate supporting small businesses, I just hate you wasting your money on something that is accessible to you for *free*. You can use templates at no cost straight from Google Docs, Canva, or Adobe Express.

HOT TIP: Whatever template you use, make sure to save the file as a PDF before you apply for anything unless specifically instructed to do otherwise. At least as of this writing, the ATS will pull data from your résumé to complete your profile in the company's system, and anything other than a PDF can often give the system troubles. An incomplete profile may mean your application doesn't go through properly, without you even knowing it.

DATA

Data is an incredibly important tool to leverage when you're writing your résumé. Data kicks ass on a résumé for two reasons:

1. Easy visualization: When recruiters are skimming your résumé, numbers pop out on the page, increasing the chances of that sentence actually getting read. In your résumé, avoid writing out a number like *one* or *two* and opt for numerals, like *1* or *2*.

2. Volume and impact: Using data is the strongest way to convey the volume of work you did and the impact of that work. When recruiters are evaluating whether you have the right level of experience for a position, it usually boils down to years of experience and volume/impact.

I recommend having at least one data point under each item of your work experience for these reasons. You might be thinking, *Girl, data? This was an entry-level job or internship. Can I just skip this part?*

Trust me, you *do* have data. If you're struggling to come up with data points, consider these questions:

- How many people did you support in your job (e.g., senior analysts you pulled reports for or managers you organized events for)?

- How many customers did you serve?

- What was the volume of the task you did (e.g., how many reports you pulled every week)?

- How many people used the product you built? How many people were impacted by your project work at the company?

See? You have data. Now throw that into the work experience sentence structure we'll discuss later in the chapter, and you're chilling.

DETAILS

Your résumé is nothing without the details of your experience. Duh. Powered by a killer design and data to help back it up, details are the most important part of all.

I firmly believe the ability to write a strong résumé is a skill you carry with you throughout your life. It's not just about the résumé. It's about your ability to break down the work you do, describe it clearly, and make sure people understand why it matters. This skill is going to help you in interviews, career conversations, and more. Oh, and I firmly believe you do not need to customize your résumé for every single application. You just need to have one well-written, absolutely gorgeous résumé to get you through.

In the next section, we'll dive into actually writing the details of your résumé.

YOUR RÉSUMÉ, FROM TOP TO BOTTOM

Now that you know your résumé needs to deliver design, data, and details, let's look at what those details should include. In this section, we'll go through each part of your résumé step-by-step, starting from the very top of your résumé and moving all the way down to the bottom.

TITLE AND CONTACT INFORMATION

Make sure your name (first and last) is clear and is the largest text on the page. Underneath that, include your phone number, email address, LinkedIn username, and a link to anything else relevant. For example, designers should include a link to their portfolio, marketers should include a link to their social media, and software engineers should include a link to their GitHub (and pleeease be actively contributing to it—trust me, managers look). Just remember never to share anything confidential or proprietary in your application. Not only can it get you into legal trouble, it also isn't good for your brand to be a corporate gossip.

PROFESSIONAL SUMMARY

The cute little introduction at the top of your résumé is called a professional summary. These are generally optional, especially if you're early in your career. Their purpose is to give a summary of your experience, set the context for the rest of your résumé, and call out what you're targeting in your next role. The professional summary can be a great opportunity to connect with the recruiter on a more personal level and have your résumé stand out. It's especially impactful if you're seeking to switch industries or functions, or make any other significant career change, as it gives you a chance to say, "Hear me out, this is why I'm great."

REALITY CHECK: A professional summary packed with buzzwords is lowkey giving "Did ChatGPT write this?" and isn't going to do you any favors. The only way the summary actually has impact is if you write it yourself. Remember, your résumé doesn't need to be packed with buzzwords to be effective. In fact, the less fluff, the better. If you're starting to itch for AI to pop in and write your résumé for you, fight it.

Your professional summary should be between three and six sentences and can be written in first or third person—just make sure it's consistent with the rest of your résumé. The old-school way of thinking is that your résumé should be written in third person, but it doesn't matter, trust me. Do whatever makes you feel the most comfortable.

The perfect formula is:

> 1 or 2 sentences to introduce who you are + 1 or 2 sentences to highlight your unique experience with a meaningful data point + 1 sentence to describe what you are looking for

Here is a template you can totally take because it doesn't sound like a robot wrote it. It sounds like a brilliant and hilarious Canadian career coach did.

> A [industry] professional with a passion for [2 or 3 things that are relevant in the job you're applying to]. With a background in [1–3 things unique to your experience], has [result of some of your work]. Actively seeking opportunities in [type of jobs you're applying to].

And here's an example of how the template might look when it's filled in:

> A finance professional with a passion for data-driven insights, strategic planning, and driving shareholder results. With a background in global financial planning, technology sales, and executive leadership, I have grown organizations' revenue by 30% and led teams of 20+ people. Actively seeking opportunities in financial leadership.

WORK EXPERIENCE

Your work experience is where you list previous jobs and your responsibilities and accomplishments at those jobs, in a way that hypes you the heck up. This makes up most of your résumé, which means it's the most important part, but also the trickiest. How can you communicate what's most important with maximum impact in such a small space?

It may shift your perspective to realize that recruiters, for the most part, don't actually understand what you do. They work with people in so many different types of jobs that they can't possibly learn all the minutiae of each one. That's why writing in clear and simple language, using data to explain *how* and *why* the work you have done matters, is going to significantly improve your résumé's performance. Basically, if your grandmother wouldn't understand what you do after reading your résumé, you've made it too complicated.

Make a List

Start by making a list of all your relevant job experience. As a rule of thumb, once you get your first full-time job, you can remove any markers of high school, including your high school graduation, volunteering, and part-time jobs. As you grow in your career, there will be past jobs that start to feel less relevant or maybe just happened a long time ago. If you're struggling to determine whether to include a given job, consider:

- Did this take place in the last ten years? If it's more than ten years old, it may be worth removing or reformatting (more to come on this latter option).

- Is the experience you gained in this role relevant to the jobs you'll be applying to? This could be related to hard skills (like technical things you've learned) or soft skills (ability to deal with people, communication, etc.). If not, you can remove it.

If you're truly stuck on a given job, leave it on, but limit how much you write about it.

Make sure your list is chronological, with the most recent experience up top and the least recent toward the bottom.

Coffee Shop Activity

Once you have a list of all your past jobs, you can start writing what you did at each job. For best results, I recommend what I call the coffee shop activity. This is an activity I do in résumé-writing sessions that has truly been the breakthrough moment for hundreds of clients.

Because, I get it, feeling like your entire career rides on the quality of a single one-page document is stressful. It feels super high-pressure and also inauthentic to list your accomplishments this way. So let's approach it in a different way.

For each work experience that you've listed, pretend you're going to grab a coffee with a friend you feel completely comfortable with. You two are catching up, and they ask you casually, "Wait, what did you even do at that job?" You wouldn't default to giving an overly structured, data-backed, corporate robot answer. You'd just chat about it like it was any other question. Here's an example:

ZAC EFRON (it's my example, let a girl have some fun): Emily, I didn't even ask. What did you do while you were an intern at the bank?

ME: Well, Zac Efron, I was an instructional design intern, so basically, I helped the senior designers build learning plans for different teams at the bank, and then I helped create the actual learning documents in their learning system and Photoshop.

Play this out in your head or record yourself on your phone answering this in the most casual, low-stress way possible. Then take bullet-point notes to capture everything you said.

My list of notes might look like this:

- I was an instructional design intern.
- I helped the senior designers build out learning plans for different teams at the bank.
- I helped create the actual learning documents in their learning system and Photoshop.

Incredible! Now I have the three main components of my job. This is the starting point.

But how do you go from scrappy notes to a well-written résumé? For each bullet point, try to answer the questions: How did I do this? Why did I do this? What was the impact of me doing this?

Let's break it down for the bullet points above.

- I helped the senior designers build out learning plans for different teams at the bank.
    - *How did I do this?* I basically did what was asked of me to collect information from different teams about what they needed training on. I put their notes into documents and files to share with the senior designers.
    - *Why did I do this?* To not get fired, but also to make sure the teams at the bank got training built for whatever their performance issues were.
    - *What was the impact of me doing this?* I ended up building three different learning programs for five hundred employees during my internship.

- I helped create the actual learning documents in their learning system and Photoshop.
  - *How did I do this?* I taught myself Photoshop and built the documents to deliver directly to the senior designers.
  - *Why did I do this?* To deliver one-pagers and learning assets for the training sessions.
  - *What was the impact of me doing this?* I ended up building three different learning programs for five hundred employees during my internship. (It's OK to have repeated info!)

Finally, imagine your friend asked you, "Was there anything else you did that was kind of random but felt like a lot of work? Maybe training new people, helping with building schedules, taking on social committee projects?" I see too many of my clients not include elements of their work experience because they weren't part of the job description, happened infrequently, or "didn't seem like a big deal." Everything you do is a big deal if you write about it like it is!

For my instructional design internship, I might tell Zac Efron:

- I was on the internship program's social committee and played a small part in organizing social events.
- I trained one of the newer interns on how to use the software and systems.

Congrats, you now have a series of somewhat disjointed notes on a page somewhere! Believe it or not, you have everything you need to write the hardest part of your résumé.

REALITY CHECK: This is where AI can be your friend. After you take a stab at working through these notes, if you're struggling to connect the dots on "Why did I do this?" and "What was the impact?" you can ask ChatGPT something like: "I worked an instructional design internship and I am working on my résumé. I am trying to make points for my résumé that explain what I worked on, why I did it, and the impact to the business/team. What impact does this have?"

Here's another example of the coffee shop exercise, this one for a retail job:

MICHAEL B. JORDAN (my other celebrity crush): Emily, love of my life, I didn't know you worked at the Gap. What was that like?

ME: Well, dear Michael, I worked retail, and I hated it. It was at Hillcrest Mall in Richmond Hill, Ontario. I just kept the store clean, sold jeans, and then went home.

MICHAEL B. JORDAN: *gets down on one knee*

Here are my notes on what I said:

- Store cleanliness/maintenance
- Sold to customers

And here's the impact of each bullet point:

- Store cleanliness/maintenance
    - *How did I do this?* I paid attention to areas in the store that were getting messy and cleaned them.
    - *Why did I do this?* To make sure the store was clean so customers could shop.
    - *What was the impact of me doing this?* It made sure customers were comfortable but also made sure there weren't safety risks with any messes.
- Sold to customers
    - *How did I do this?* I met customers one-on-one to understand what they were shopping for, communicated any discounts, and then helped them pick items out.
    - *Why did I do this?* To drive sales and help people.
    - *What was the impact of me doing this?* I sold to probably ten people a day, which contributed to store revenue.

And finally, here's the miscellaneous stuff I didn't initially include:

- Sometimes I would help close the tills and shadow the store manager on administrative tasks.
- I also trained new employees.

If you're feeling super stuck or like you can't remember what you did at this job (maybe you blacked it out because it was that horrible), you can always google job postings for the same title (at that company or a different one) to get a reminder of the tasks you may be forgetting. You don't ever want to copy and paste a job description into your résumé, but it may trigger some memories of tasks you carried out.

And now that your coffee shop exercise is complete, you can start putting the notes to use by turning them into well-structured sentences.

Structure Your Sentences

I've looked at thousands of résumés in my life, and every single good résumé has this in common: Every work experience should start with a summary sentence as the first bullet point on the résumé.

The formula for the perfect résumé is to start each entry in your work experience with a strong summary sentence. Then follow up with two to five bullet points breaking down the core responsibilities of your work as demonstrated with results. The easiest sentence structure to follow for each bullet point is this:

> [action verb] in doing [tasks] impacting/delivered to/ supporting/resulting in [data]

Here's what that looks like in action for my experience as an instructional design intern:

- Supported a team of 5 instructional designers in developing and delivering end-to-end learning programs for the Canadian corporate banking teams, including onboarding and compliance training.

- Consulted with business leaders to collect information on their learning needs and presented findings to senior designers.

- Partnered with senior designers to create infographics, video, and text-based learning materials, delivered to 500+ employees.

- Sat on the Intern Social Committee as a member to plan 3 social events over the course of the summer, including a mixer lunch, networking dinner, and ice-skating.

And here's what it looks like for my experience at the Gap:

- Delivered exceptional customer experiences through consultative sales, merchandising, and store administration.

- Worked one-on-one with customers to understand their needs and generate sales for the store, serving 10+ customers per day and generating $900 of sales per shift.

- Supported in-store administration to ensure accurate reporting and loss prevention, including balancing tills, making schedules, and managing health and safety activities.

- Trained and mentored new hires to ensure a consistent experience for customers.

Giving Your Experience Weight

One of the biggest mistakes people make in their résumé is they tend to downplay their experiences. I often hear clients say things like "Well, it wasn't a big deal," "That was just a small part of my job," or "I just helped on the project."

Enough of this. I get that sitting down to put together a highly scrutinized document designed to summarize your experience while simultaneously boasting about every win you've ever had is . . . uncomfy. But the goal here is not comfort. The goal is getting paid! And the people who get paid are the ones who are able to clearly highlight their experiences with a sense of pride. So, effective immediately, stop shrinking your experiences. Operate like every single thing you do matters, because it does.

From a résumé-writing perspective, one of the easiest ways to demonstrate your contributions and highlight your work is to start each bullet point with an action verb that puts you in the center of the action. You can write either entirely in present tense or write everything in past tense except for your current job. (Writing your current role in past tense gets confusing.) Here's a list of my all-time favorite action verbs, broken down by category:

- Leadership and collaboration: Led, Managed, Coordinated, Executed, Facilitated, Trained

- Project management and strategy: Developed, Designed, Implemented, Launched, Streamlined, Organized, Documented

- Problem-solving and analytical thinking: Analyzed, Diagnosed, Evaluated, Investigated, Researched, Collected

- Communication: Presented, Facilitated, Partnered with, Advised

- Sales and customer service: Sold, Promoted, Upsold, Advised, Assisted, Supported, Served

- Technical: Programmed, Engineered, Debugged, Automated
- Finance and data: Audited, Budgeted, Forecasted, Reconciled, Processed, Calculated, Analyzed, Modeled
- Creative and marketing: Designed, Conceptualized, Illustrated, Composed, Wrote, Edited, Branded, Advertised, Optimized, Storyboarded
- Administrative and operations: Organized, Processed, Scheduled, Executed, Managed, Standardized, Maintained

The Finishing Touches

After you've run this exercise for each item in your work experience, step away. Go get a real coffee with a friend who isn't imaginary. And then come back to reread what you have. You know when you look at something for so long, you either start to nitpick and find a million things wrong with it, or, conversely, you think it's a work of art only to realize later it still needs a lot of work? Let's not.

Come back to your résumé with fresh eyes, and I challenge you to read it as if you had no idea what you did for work and ask yourself the following questions:

- Is the purpose of each job clear?
- Is the impact of each job clear?
- Is the volume of work done in each job clear?
- Are my technical and nontechnical skills clear?

If yes, you're off to the races. If not, give it another go.

EDUCATION SECTION

Whew! We made it through the hard part! Now we're on to a much easier section of your résumé: your education. Here's where you list the university you graduated from and the degree you earned. You can also list any certificates, trade school education, associate degrees, or more. If you have multiple degrees (look at you, smarty pants!), you can simply follow the same format below and include each. If you are a new graduate, you can leave on your GPA, graduation year, or any other affiliations—but after you land your first gig, drop them. It's a marker of your youth (jealous) and people may not consider you for senior roles because of it.

Remember, if you're a student or new grad, you're allowed to put this at the top of your résumé, although I tend to advise leaving it at the bottom if you have sufficient experience (think anything beyond three years). Your education section ideally shouldn't be taking up too much real estate. I would recommend something like this:

> Bachelor of Human Resources Management,
> York University
>
> *(3.9, Notable courses: Employment Law [A] and Compensation [A+])*

See, I told you the hard part was done.

ADDITIONAL INFORMATION

Finally, we arrive at the last (and most fun!) section of your résumé: additional information. So few people talk about the power of this section on a résumé. But having worked with thousands of hiring managers and HR professionals, I can tell you this section is *the* conversation starter. Think of it as an opportunity to clearly outline your technical skills and any other interesting facts that make you stand out as a candidate. In this wildly competitive job market, having a section that makes you a *person* with a *personality* is going to change the game.

Remember, almost everyone else is using ChatGPT or online templates to write their résumé. They all sound the same. But you? You're built different.

Remember those work experiences that weren't super relevant but that may be good indicators of your personality or a subject that is important to you? Those can totally live here, too.

I advise structuring your additional information section like this:

- Technical skills: List software you use, coding languages, spoken languages, processes you're used to, etc. Avoid listing things that everyone knows like Microsoft Office products and email.

- Volunteering: List any volunteering, school committees, etc.

- Additional interests: List a few things here that showcase what you like to do outside of work but that still make you look smart. For example, list podcasts or books aligned with your field, public speakers, or other activities deemed productive by society.

- Additional work experience: You could list the less relevant but still interesting work experience here.

Here's a killer example of an additional information section:

Additional Experience: Fashion blogging at SHE Canada Magazine, serving at Harbor 60 Restaurant

Personal Interests: *Listening to personal development podcasts (*Diary of a CEO*), reading (*Clock In*), volunteering (Toronto Humane Society), and long-distance running*

THE COVER LETTER

Now you know how to write a killer résumé, but while a résumé is the most important part of the job application, it's not the only part. There's also the cover letter—sort of. I'm going to hold your hand as I tell you this, but no one is reading your cover letter. I used to spend hours writing what some called "the most beautiful cover letter of all time" and "a poignant tour de force," only to start working as a recruiter and realize that no one actually reads those things. It makes no sense! Why are people asking for them if they aren't even being evaluated?!

Alas, it's how things work. The relevance of cover letters truly boils down to industry. In more old-school industries, operate under the assumption that you need a cover letter for every single application (while retaining the wisdom that no one is reading it). In newer-school industries, it's not as common for a company to request a cover letter with your application, and you really only need to use one when it's requested.

But regardless of the industry, attaching a cover letter is never going to hurt your chances of getting an interview. If anything, it can be helpful, even if it's not strictly necessary. I just don't want you pouring hours into this thing, because chances are, it's getting skimmed—not read.

Here's a template to help you produce a high-quality cover letter with minimal time and effort:

Dear [name of company, name of hiring manager, or "hiring team"],

I am [name], a [job title or student status] passionate about [2 or 3 things relevant in your industry]. I am reaching out to express my interest in the [job title] role at [company]. With [number] years of experience in [2 or 3 things they call out in the job description], I have a track record of [something you're known for].

In my current role at [current job, student status, or most recent internship], I had the opportunity to [1 or 2 things you did], resulting in [impact]. Prior to this, I worked at [role you had before this, previous internship, or school project], where I was able to [1 or 2 things you did].

I am deeply excited to submit my application for this role, as my experience in [what you do], coupled with my passion for [something the company listed in their values on their careers webpage], is a strong fit.

Thank you for considering my application. I look forward to the possibility of discussing this exciting opportunity with you.

Thanks,
[name]

When the template is filled in, it might look something like this:

Dear Hiring Team,

I am Valeria Gutiérrez, a software developer passionate about building meaningful products, scalable code, and innovation. I am reaching out to express my interest in the staff software developer role at Google. With 8+ years of experience in full-stack development and team leadership, I have a track record of contributing to industry-leading consumer products that impact 4 million customers globally.

In my current role at Amazon, I had the opportunity to lead the end-to-end development of a new streaming app, including requirement gathering, cross-functional partnerships, and deployment resulting in more than $2 million in revenue. Prior to this, I worked at a tech startup as a back-end development lead, managing a team of 4 engineers, where I was able to work in a fast-paced environment to offer engineering services to a variety of clients.

I am deeply excited to submit my application for this role, as my experience in full-stack development and people leadership, coupled with my passion for innovation and collaboration, is a strong fit.

Thank you for considering my application. I look forward to the possibility of discussing this exciting opportunity with you.

Sincerely,
Valeria Gutiérrez

Damn. I'd hire the hell out of her.

LEARN TO LOVE LINKEDIN

Finally, before you start applying for jobs, you need to update your LinkedIn. Trust me. They're looking.

LinkedIn launched in 2003, and truly, NWTS (nothing was the same). It operates as both a digital résumé and a digital business card when networking with people. It's also the number one platform that recruiters use to proactively source for talent and do some additional creeping of any candidates they are considering.

Over one billion people use LinkedIn, and there are six people hired every minute on the platform. Roughly 72 percent of recruiters use LinkedIn when they're searching for new talent. So if you're on the fence about whether or not you need a profile, or if you should invest in updating yours, get off the fence. You need a well-crafted LinkedIn profile, full stop.

How does LinkedIn work? First of all, there are actually two versions of LinkedIn: the normal one you use, and the behind-the-scenes one employers and recruiters use, which is called LinkedIn Recruiter. (The crowd lets out an excited "Ooh, aah!") Think of LinkedIn Recruiter as the back-end search function of the LinkedIn that you're used to using. Effectively, this version of LinkedIn offers interesting industry insights, analytics on the job market, and of course, advanced search options for candidates—the latter being the feature recruiters use most.

When a recruiter gets assigned a new position to fill, typically they first review any inbound applications in the ATS, which, as you now know, is the internal system every company uses to collect job applications. (Whether you apply for a job on LinkedIn or another platform, your application will always be routed to the company's ATS for review.)

But sometimes none of the applications in the ATS are exactly what a company is looking for. Just because job postings that previously received one hundred applicants are now getting upwards of one thousand doesn't mean those applicants are actually a perfect fit for the position. This means that, especially for more niche roles, recruiters often have to take to LinkedIn and do some headhunting.

On the recruiter's side of LinkedIn, there are several fields we can use to search for candidates, including:

- Location
- Job title
- Length of time in current role
- Seniority
- Open to work
- Hybrid, remote, in office
- Previous employers
- Skills
- Key words

Even if some LinkedIn features change in the future (or if another job website takes over the first-place spot someday), it's safe to say that these are the kinds of things recruiters will always be searching for when looking at candidates. And knowing what recruiters are searching for will let you build your profile in a way that ensures not only that you come up in searches but that you're on the first page of search results, baby! LinkedIn Recruiter effectively works like a Google search, so a great LinkedIn profile is going to be optimized in a way that makes sure you're getting noticed.

Optimizing your profile may sound difficult, but truly it is very simple. It means you need to ensure each of the above sections, like your photo, header, title, biography, work experience, education, and key words are all filled out. Having a complete profile is half the battle.

The other half is using words that recruiters typically search for. The first thing you should do is search up a job posting online for a job you really want and look at the key words used in that posting. For example, if you search "medical device sales manager," you'll see postings with words like *collaboration, end-to-end sales, sales force, CRM, values-based selling*, etc. These are the key words you want to ensure are included in your list of skills, your biography, and your work experience. The second thing you can do is ask your AI platform of choice what key words you should add and to double-check if you've missed any. It's that easy.

YOUR DIGITAL FOOTPRINT

LinkedIn isn't the only website you need to be mindful of. Most employers admit to searching candidates on Google before interviews and before they make job offers. So make your social media accounts private while job hunting, or at least stop posting slutty edits of your favorite TV characters.

Things that are OK on social media from an employer's POV:

- Photos of your friends and family
- You being at social events, including parties
- Photos of you with a drink in your hand
- Photos of you dressed in your weekend clothes

Things that are not OK on social media from an employer's POV:

- You being a weird internet bully, troll, or general asshole
- Hardcore heavy drinking and drugs (a photo of you holding a pint of beer is fine; a photo of you doing a keg stand is probably not)
- You speaking ill of your previous employers online

We've all heard the stories of people getting offers taken away or even fired because of posts on social media. And on first listen, it can sound scary. But truly, if you use common sense with what you post, you'll be just fine.

BRINGING IT ALL TOGETHER

Congratulations! With the tools you've acquired in this chapter, you're ready to create the best version of your cover letter, your LinkedIn, and most importantly, your résumé. Once you've got your solid-gold application ready to roll, how can you make sure it reaches the right people and gives you the best shot at the job you want? See you in the next chapter.

CHAPTER 5

MAKE YOUR NETWORK WORK

Now that you know how the hiring process works and have a stellar résumé in your back pocket, you're ready to apply for jobs. You may have applied for jobs before, but trust me, you haven't done it like this. Effective immediately, your job-search strategy has two parts: flagging your application *and* actively networking to garner referrals. Both prongs of your job-search strategy are equally important, so let's dig in. This chapter is a comprehensive guide to applying for jobs online while tapping into and building a network.

FLAGGING YOUR APPLICATION

Let's start with the easier of the two prongs: applying directly to jobs online. To be clear, this isn't the job market your parents grew up with, or even the job market I experienced ten years ago. This is something much worse. Far more evil. Back in my day, you could apply for a job, and if you were qualified . . . someone would probably get back to you for an interview. If you weren't qualified . . . someone would take thirty seconds to decline your application.

We don't live in that world anymore. The job market is so saturated that getting any response to your application, even if it's a rejection, feels like an Olympic sport.

The challenge in today's market isn't just having a perfect résumé, it's getting someone to open your résumé in the first place. So yes, you're going to apply online for jobs, but you're also going to reach out and flag your application every single time. This is the exact step-by-step formula I give my clients when they're looking for jobs.

STEP 1:
APPLY

When you see a job you like, apply for it online. Don't waste your time following viral "hacks" by only applying on certain days of the week or at certain times of day. It's not making a difference. Craft your résumé like I taught you in chapter 4 and apply.

STEP 2:
FIND YOUR FUTURE NETWORK

Immediately after you apply for the job, go to LinkedIn and search up the following people at the company you just applied to: someone who's currently in the role you applied to, a manager for the role you applied to, and a recruiter. Your searches on LinkedIn will look like this:

a. "[job title] manager [company]"

b. "[job title you applied to] [company]"

c. "recruiter [company]"

So, for example, if you just applied to be a financial analyst at KPMG, your searches would look like:

a. "finance manager KPMG" or "senior finance manager KPMG"

b. "financial analyst KPMG" or "finance analyst KPMG"

c. "recruiter KPMG"

This search should pull up at least three to six people. Pay attention to how long they've been there (if it's a couple of years, that's usually a good sign they don't hate the company), if they've announced that they're quitting in a LinkedIn post (probably a bad idea to reach out to that person), and where they're located (it should typically be the same place you're located unless the job is fully remote).

STEP 3: REACH OUT TO THE CONTACTS

Every single time you apply for a job, reach out to at least three people on this list with the below script:

> Hi [contact], I'm [name], a [job title] at [company] (or student at [school]). I wanted to reach out to flag my application for the [job title] role. I see you've been at [company] for [amount of time] and would love to pick your brain to learn more about your experience and potentially the position, if you may be open to a quick call or chat exchange. Thank you!

STEP 4: SCHEDULE A CHAT

The goal of reaching out in this way is for at least one of these people to respond (sounds like my goal on Bumble, tbh). In their response, they'll ideally offer to speak to you on the phone to chat more about their experience and the role, offer to connect you to the hiring team via email, or even offer to refer you directly. You can customize the outreach if you like, but really the call to action is what matters here. You aren't begging them for a referral. You're simply asking to learn more about them and drawing attention to your application. They have control over how they respond, and any of these responses can help you stand out.

REALITY CHECK: Asking someone for a referral right out of the gate when they don't even know you is . . . probably not the best way to go about this. What we do know, based on psychology, is that people love to talk about themselves, especially when it comes to their career. Which is why framing your ask like "I'd love to pick your brain and learn from you" is going to get you further than "Give me a referral, internet stranger."

This may sound like an ungodly amount of work to do for each and every job application. It kind of is. I don't think this is fair and equitable, but I do think it is what it is. The more you commit to this process, the sooner you get hired. Based on the volume of roles you're applying to, you may need to consider purchasing LinkedIn Premium, as standard LinkedIn caps the number of notes you can send out at one time, at least as of this writing. I personally vote for trying to apply without spending money and then seeing if it becomes a need later on.

PHONE A FRIEND

Another incredible hack for after you apply for a job is to tap into your current network to ask for a referral in a direct (but ultimately kind of sneaky) way. There are two options for how to do this:

1. If you know anyone who works at the company (LinkedIn should show you "Connections who work here" on the job application page), feel free to shoot them a note that reads: "Hi [name], I hope you've been doing well! I wanted to reach out because I saw that you're working at [company], and I recently applied for the [job title] role that was posted. I'd love to connect and hear about your experience there!"

2. If you don't have any direct connections who work at this company, you can ask around to see if your friends, professors, or family know anyone who does. From there, you can ask to be connected to the relevant employee via email and send a similar note to the one in option 1. With any of these reach-outs, the goal is to get the person on the phone for fifteen minutes. (I'll drop the secrets on why in just a sec.)

There are also websites where you can pay someone to send in a referral for you, but I don't recommend them. One could argue they're unethical because the referral isn't genuine, of course, but beyond that, they create an unequal playing field that disadvantages candidates who don't have the money to pay for referrals. Also, you aren't making genuine connections at the company, so it doesn't help you long-term. And getting a referral in the company system means significantly less than having a chat with someone at the company. For these reasons, I'd say to avoid these kinds of websites.

HOW DO REFERRALS WORK?

Welcome to part two of your strategy. If you're actively looking for a job, you need to be flagging your application every time you apply somewhere, either with people in your network or people that you've found on LinkedIn. But in addition to that, you need to be proactively expanding your existing network.

There is no excuse not to network. Networking is the best way to get referrals, and you need those today, and ten years from now, and twenty years from now. Referrals are often more likely to pass recruiter reviews, and nearly 80 percent of jobs are filled by word of mouth.

Of course, referrals work best when your mom or dad is the CEO at the company, because then they can simply call the recruiter and force them to find (or make up) a job for an underqualified but well-connected candidate. Assuming you didn't win that particular networking lottery, this book is a close second. (Just try to marry rich as a backup.)

The personal connection you make by networking gets you further today, but it also adds more people to your network who you can potentially reach out to again in the future for mentorship or referrals. If you don't already have a preexisting network, we are going to make you one.

MAKE A NETWORK THAT WORKS FOR YOU

Everybody and their mother preaches the importance of networking, and they're right. The issue with networking as we know it is that the advice you've been given is probably dated and awkward. There's a better way to build connections that doesn't feel as labor intensive and that yields better results. By the time you finish this chapter, you'll make networking a part of your life and habits forever. Well, at least until you retire. Ideally, you should be networking on an ongoing basis, but your efforts for sure need to ramp up if you're actively job hunting.

Here's exactly what you're going to do:

1. Remember the jobs you're interested in from the Your Hit List exercise in chapter 1? Search those babies up on LinkedIn and see what companies are hiring for them.

2. From that list, determine the top twenty companies you're interested in working for that offer jobs in your field. Feel free to throw in companies that aren't actively hiring if that isn't the stage you're at right now.

3. Then search "[job title] manager [company]" and "[job title] [company]" on LinkedIn. You'll get a list of people who either manage the roles you're targeting or are currently in those roles.

4. Reach out and ask for a career conversation with this script: "Hi [name], I'm [name], a [what you do] who is passionate about [something that ties into the work you do]. I wanted to reach out to see if you may be open to a quick career conversation, as I'd love to learn more about your experience at [something that stands out on their profile]. I'm happy to book a quick phone call or chat online, whatever is best for you. Thank you."

Notice how this reach-out isn't specifically about a job that you're interested in. The goal of networking is to establish relationships that you maintain over the course of your career and identify potential mentors. The reason this is so important is that the more people you network with, the more you have a community who is willing to refer you to jobs, connect you to new opportunities, and give you advice or perspective as needed. Reaching out to flag your application is the short-term play; networking is the long-term one.

HOT TIP: For every ten messages you send on LinkedIn, expect one response. The response rate will be low, and that's OK. All it takes is one person to change the game.

MASTERING THE ART OF THE CAREER CONVERSATION

The goal of all this application flagging and networking is to get these people on a phone or video call. That's because you're undeniably lovable; they just need to talk to you to understand that. You want to be more than a piece of paper. These conversations transition you from being a candidate to being a *person they know.* It's different.

So, let's say the person you reached out to responds and says they're open to speaking. Great! Except, now, like . . . you do have to speak to them.

Don't panic. Old-school advice would tell you to treat this conversation like an interview, to come in hot and ask for what you want. This can work in theory, but in practice, it's likely going to feel uncomfortable and will therefore be ineffective.

Good news: We don't do old school around here. I'm going to walk you through exactly how to have an effective career conversation.

STEP 1:
SEND AN INVITE

Send a proper thirty-minute calendar hold to the person you're meeting with, including a video conferencing link or phone number. Make the subject of the email "Connection: [your name] x [their name]" and write in the body: "Thank you in advance for your time. I'm looking forward to learning more about your career in [company or industry]."

STEP 2:
CREEP THEIR LINKEDIN

This is the only time (that I will admit to) that being an internet creep is entirely acceptable. Head to the person's LinkedIn profile and make some bulleted notes about where they went to school, what work experiences they have, and anything else interesting you may see.

STEP 3:
PREPARE QUESTIONS

Write a list of three to five questions based on the notes you've taken about the person's LinkedIn, specific to learning about *them*. Some of my favorites include:

- Were you always passionate about [industry/job]?
- How did you break into the industry?
- What was your experience like when transitioning from [company A] to [company B]?
- Is there anything you wish you could go back and tell yourself when you first started in this role?

- What would you say are the hard and soft skills that set you up for success in your career?

- During your time at [company], have there been any projects or achievements that you're very excited by?

- I'd love to hear more about your day-to-day in your role. What is that like for you?

- What are some of the challenges you and your team have worked through recently?

- How do you see the future of your industry in light of [global event you're knowledgeable on]?

- Is there any advice you would give someone starting their career in this industry?

STEP 4: PREPARE YOUR CONVERSATION OUTLINE

Map out the general flow of the conversation you expect to have—or borrow mine! I don't mind.

YOU: Hi, [name]! How are you? Thank you again for your time!

THEM: My pleasure!

YOU: I would love to use this time to learn more about your career. Part of why I reached out to you specifically is because of [something that is true but also boosts their ego]. Maybe I can start off with a quick introduction of myself for context, and then I would love to hear about your career journey!

> *- This works because you're setting the intention and taking control of the conversation. It shows you won't waste their time. There's nothing worse than someone who doesn't prepare for career chats.*

THEM: Sure!

YOU: Great! I'm [name], and I'm a [job title/student status]. I'm super passionate about [career-related things you love to do that relate to this person]. Over the last several years, I've been doing [work or school accomplishments], and I've now shifted my focus to [your goal for this chat, e.g., learning more about careers in your shared industry].

> *- Notice how you're saying "learning about" careers? This comes off as much less demanding. You're simply trying to learn from this person. You aren't asking for favors or referrals, which can be off-putting so early in a conversation. Trust me, this language works.*

THEM: (Introduces their own career journey.)

YOU: (Based on how much time you have, ask the questions you wrote in step 3.)

> *- The best way to shine here is to actively listen. Genuinely listen to what they're saying, take authentic interest, and react naturally. Don't worry about performing and being seen as an active listener. Be yourself, listen to what they have to say, and respond when it makes sense. You'll riff a little here.*

YOU: This is great, thank you! Do you happen to have any questions for me?

THEM: (May or may not ask questions.)

YOU: Thank you so much, this has been so helpful. I was wondering, if you're comfortable, may I . . .

> - *. . . reach back out in a couple of months to continue learning from you? (Ask this if your goal is mentorship.)*
>
> - *. . . stay connected in case there are any opportunities in your network or organization that may be a good fit for me? (Ask this if you want a referral or job.)*
>
> - *. . . ask if there's anyone in your network you advise I connect with? (Ask this if you want to expand your network.)*

THEM: (Will say yes or no. Usually the answer is yes.)

FOLLOWING UP

So you followed the steps above and had a great career conversation. Mission accomplished, right? Wrong. This is where so many people stop. And then they wonder why networking isn't working for them. Well, it's because you've just planted the seed! You don't harvest the fruit the same day you plant the seed, you little gardener. If you want the seed to keep growing, the day after your conversation, you're going to send a follow-up email to the person you spoke to. The script you use will vary depending on what you want.

IF YOU WANT MENTORSHIP

If you want mentorship, your script will look like this:

Hi [name],

Thank you again for your time yesterday. I so enjoyed our conversation and learning more about [something you learned about].

As mentioned, I would love to continue learning from your experience if that's something you might be open to. If so, I would be more than happy to send a calendar hold sometime in the month of [a month that is at least a bit in the future].

Best,
[your name]

Why this works: This is a more casual way of saying "Will you mentor me?" If you want to keep learning from this person, just keep sending emails like this. By the way, this is all mentorship is: ongoing chats with someone you trust. Sometimes people try to overcomplicate or formalize the idea of mentorship. Don't. Meet someone you respect, connect with them regularly, and boom, a mentor is born.

IF YOU WANT A POSTED JOB

If you want a job that has already been posted at this person's company, use this script:

Hi [name],

Thank you again for your time yesterday. I so enjoyed our conversation and learning more about [something you learned about].

As mentioned, I've been actively thinking about next steps in my career and wanted to flag that I've applied to this job posting [insert the link]. After our conversation, I feel even more inclined to apply. I wanted to reach out to see if you happen to know who is running the recruitment process on this.

Thank you,
[your name]

Why this works: This is a less aggressive way of asking for a referral. You've already applied for the job, which shows you aren't expecting anything from this person—you're just asking to be connected to the recruitment team. Ideally, they'll email the recruiter with a personal recommendation or connect the two of you for a career chat (which you're already an expert at).

IF YOU WANT A JOB BUT DON'T SEE ONE POSTED

If you want a job at this person's company but don't see one you like that has been posted, use this script:

Hi [name],

Thank you again for your time yesterday. I so enjoyed our conversation and learning more about [something you learned about].

As mentioned, I've been actively thinking about next steps in my career and would love to stay connected should there be any roles that are a good fit at your organization or in your network.

Thank you again!
[your name]

Why this works: You're encouraging connection and ongoing conversation with this person, which may prompt them to connect you to a friend or, at a minimum, keep you top of mind for them.

IF YOU WANT TO BE CONNECTED TO PEOPLE IN THEIR NETWORK

If you want to expand your own network by connecting to others in this person's network, use this script:

Hi [name],

Thank you again for your time yesterday. I so enjoyed our conversation and learning more about [something you learned about].

As mentioned, I would love to stay close to you and potentially be connected with anyone you suggest in your network!

Thank you again,
[your name]

Why this works: This one's pretty straightforward, no?

KEEP YOUR NETWORK WORKING

Now you know the fundamentals of networking! If you invest in a network today, it will benefit you for the rest of your career.

The secret sauce to networking is keeping your network warm while also deciding who to focus on. You don't need to keep in touch with every single person you connect with. Like with anything in life, you may not hit it off with everyone. Maybe their experience doesn't benefit you from a learning perspective, or maybe you two just didn't click. It's OK to simply send a thank-you email and never speak to them again.

But for the people you would like to keep around, you need to make a conscious effort to do so. I would argue that reaching out every two to four months for the first year is great, and even less frequently than that as time goes on. This ensures the people you connect with actually feel like you're taking the time to invest in a relationship with them, that it isn't transactional. And it keeps you top of mind for any opportunities they come across. These keep-warm reach-outs don't even need to be conversations if you don't feel like that will be necessary. You can try these strategies:

- Send a seasonal email to see how their fall/winter/summer/spring was.
- Send over an article relevant to topics you two have discussed that may be of interest.
- Share a progress update on advice or action items they gave you.
- Send an invitation for another chat if needed, following a similar structure to the ones you've already used in this chapter. But over time, you'll become much more comfortable with one another and can ditch the outlines and just speak like colleagues.
- Reach out when you see a job posted that you're interested in at their company.

Treat the people you network with like distant friends who you catch up with every now and again, and occasionally ask for favors as needed. It's pretty chill.

Remember, some good jobs are online, but most are hidden in this secret job market powered by networking. Almost 80 percent of jobs get filled by word of mouth. Networking is the way word gets out.

SO WHAT'S YOUR GAME PLAN?

If your goal is to get a new job ASAP, the more roles you apply for, the better. The same goes for networking: The more you do, the faster the process moves. I would say aim for twenty or more applications and one to three career chats per week if you're serious about things moving quickly. If you're not in a hurry, or are just looking to expand your network, one new contact a month is more than fine! Networking is a marathon, not a sprint.

Listen, I get it. This is a shit ton of work. You've gotta update your résumé and LinkedIn, apply for jobs, follow up on those applications, *and* network. This is a full-time job in itself! Job application burnout is real, especially when there's financial or timing pressure on you. To avoid losing your ever-loving mind, I suggest adopting a shift work schedule for your job search.

MONDAY	Check for new jobs in the a.m. with your coffee. 5–6 p.m.: Apply for jobs intentionally and flag your application.
TUESDAY	Check for new jobs in the a.m. with your coffee. 5–6 p.m.: Apply for jobs intentionally and flag your application.
WEDNESDAY	Check for new jobs in the a.m. with your coffee.
THURSDAY	Check for new jobs in the a.m. with your coffee. 5–6 p.m.: Reach out to existing network or reach out to people for career chats on LinkedIn.
FRIDAY	Check for new jobs in the a.m. with your coffee. 1–2 p.m.: Have one career chat.
SATURDAY	REST.
SUNDAY	REST.

Of course, this isn't the only schedule structure that can work for you, but dividing the labor into shifts with designated rest days can make this feel much more manageable.

With all of this incredible networking, I know you're going to get interviews. Should we prep?

CHAPTER 6

INTERVIEW BOOT CAMP

So you nailed your application, networked flawlessly, and, surprise, you landed a job interview! If you're anything like me, you're equal parts excited and terrified. After all, interviews are intimidating.

But what if I told you that interviewing is a muscle you can grow, just like your glutes? Great news: I've perfected both. However, I'm only qualified to talk about one. So sit your glutes down. I'm about to tell you how to *never* feel nervous or flop in an interview ever again. This chapter is the ultimate resource on how to prepare for an interview like a literal pro.

RECRUITERS AND CONFIRMATION BIAS

Just in case you forgot, if you've been selected for an interview, it's because the recruiter thinks you're qualified. It's as simple as that. You're being invited into the interview process because they like what they see.

Contrary to popular belief, recruiters are humans, too. And humans really don't like being wrong, which is why they cling to confirmation bias. Confirmation bias is a thing all human brains tend to do; they look for evidence to support their preexisting beliefs.

Even on a subconscious level, the recruiter is looking for evidence to prove to themselves that they were right all along and that you are, in fact, the person for the job.

Working on the human resources floor in a cubicle next to dozens of other recruiters, I'd hear *a lot* of info: which hiring manager pissed off the finance team, which team's budget was getting cut, and so on. But the thing I heard recruiters say before nearly every interview was always the same: "God, I hope they do well."

My dear friend, at least part of the fear you feel about interviews will start to fade the moment you accept that the recruiter actually wants to see you do well. Remind yourself of this:

- The recruiter picked you to move forward in the process, so if you do poorly, they look like they aren't good at their job.

- Recruiter performance is literally evaluated based on their ability to fill positions with good candidates. Hiring you is the goal of their job.

- Many recruiters actually get paid a commission when they hire someone, so you getting this job gets them paid.

Trust me, they want to see you do well. Take a breath. This is a conversation, not an interrogation, and everyone here wants to see you shine.

OK, but what does "shining" look like? Spoiler: It's not two creepy twins in nightgowns following you around a deserted hotel.

Shining in the context of an interview means you're feeding the interviewer what they want to hear. Most interview processes have at least two rounds, and if you want to work as a software engineer at a big tech company, there could be as many as seven. But at each round in the interview process, the interviewer is assessing for two core things:

1. Skills: Do you have the technical skills and experience to complete this job well?

2. Values: Does your communication style and way of working align with the organization's?

Your job is to make sure you communicate how you check both of those boxes in the interview. My job is to teach you how.

ACTION: Stop feeling like everyone wants to see you fail. And maybe watch *The Shining* if you didn't get my reference earlier.

WHAT TO EXPECT IN EACH INTERVIEW

We're about to get super practical on interview prep. Every industry and company is different, but as a rule of thumb, this is what you can expect in each round of interviewing.

INTERVIEW ROUND	INTERVIEWER	WHAT TO EXPECT
First (Prescreen)	Recruiter	• Introduction of who you are • Why you're looking for a new role/ why you've applied to this role • 2–5 higher-level questions about your skills and values

INTERVIEW ROUND	INTERVIEWER	WHAT TO EXPECT
Second	Hiring manager or team member	• Introduction of who you are (again, lol) • Why you're interested in the role/company, especially after learning more in the prescreen • 2–5 more niche questions about your skills and values • Questions like "What would you do to solve [X problem]?"
Third (Technical)	Hiring manager or team member	• This is usually for technical roles like software engineers and data analysts; you may be given a case study or project to work on and demonstrate your technical skills
Final	Hiring manager or a panel	• The more senior the role, the more likely you will have a final-round panel-style interview • Often these include a take-home case study you will present or a live problem to solve and present to the team

The details of the interview steps can vary, so it's totally normal to ask the recruiter what to expect in the next round of interviews and how many steps there are in the process.

HOW TO PREPARE FOR ANY INTERVIEW

Now that you know the general layout of the interview process, it's time to start your prep. The reality is it's hard to ace an interview you haven't prepared for. With my step-by-step instructions, you'll be ready to face any interview, at any stage, with calm and confidence.

STEP 1: SMALL TALK IS A BIG DEAL

Fifty percent of employers say that they know if a candidate is a good fit for the job in the first five minutes of the interview. Is that because they took the time to properly ask you questions and get to know you super quickly? Of course not. In those five minutes, the employer is making assumptions about you based on first impressions. One of the biggest contributors to your first impression? Small talk.

The biggest mistake that candidates make in interviews is they skip the small talk. They want to get right to business. Girl, small talk is corporate foreplay. You need it. When the interview starts, either in person or virtually, start the conversation with a warm hello, thank them for having you, and either ask how they are *or* when they ask how you're doing, actually give them something to work with. Too often, I see candidates respond to "How are you?" with "Good! You?" Boring! Boooo!

The employer has received hundreds or even thousands of applications, remember? At any given stage of the interview process, I can almost guarantee they're interviewing at least four other people. Your superpower isn't a perfect résumé—it's the fact that no one else is *you*. So when the interviewer asks how you are, reply with something positive that opens up the door for conversation and highlights your personality.

So, how are you?

- "I'm well, thank you! I had a great morning walking the dog and tried a new coffee spot, so I had a nice start to the day. How about you?"

- "I'm great, thank you! I had a super restful evening watching that new Netflix series called [trending, non-raunchy show], so I feel good!"

Catch my drift? Tell them you aren't just good, you're *great*, and then give them a high-level reason *why*. This shows you're a good conversationalist, which means you're easy to work with. Plus, you open up the door for them to banter with you a little. Ideally, the recruiter will ask a follow-up question or share a bit about their own day. This is so powerful because it makes you more than just another candidate; it makes you a person. It breaks the ice, helps eliminate some of your anxiety, and really sets the tone. "This candidate . . . can hang!" the interviewer will say in awe.

STEP 2: PREPARE AN INTRODUCTION

In almost every interview you have for the rest of your life, you will be asked to "tell me a bit about yourself" or "walk me through your experience." This is partly because many recruiters are lazy and haven't read your résumé, but it's also because they want to hear how you communicate. The reasoning doesn't matter. What matters is that you never have to get ready if you stay ready. Having a strong, attention-commanding way of introducing yourself is a good thing when you're networking in real life, chatting in the office with new people, and of course interviewing. You'll use this format for the rest of your career, trust me.

Now, people are generally pretty short on attention span, so try to keep your introduction to under two minutes. Honestly, even two minutes is pushing it.

Ideally, you're structuring your introduction with:

- 1 or 2 sentences describing who you are and what you do

- 2 to 4 sentences calling out your passion powered by your achievements
- 1 or 2 sentences on why you're interested in this position at this specific company

For example, mine might be something like this:

I'm Emily, a principal recruiter with experience in developing international recruitment strategies for internship- to executive-level roles in industries like technology, investment banking, and marketing. I'm passionate about delivering career-changing candidate experiences and building strategies that power diversity, equity, and inclusion at organizations. During my time at [X company], I was responsible for raising the percentage of women in engineering from 20 percent to 37 percent in less than one year. Part of this includes recruitment marketing campaigns that I have led in partnership with PR organizations for both digital and in-person experiences with a reach of over 3 million. When I saw this role posted, I was super excited. I saw the ask for international-level recruitment experience and a need to have a marketing edge, which is aligned both with my experience and with what I love to do. Plus, [company's] commitment to [something from their website] really excited me.

See how this called out skills *and* values? Brilliant.

STEP 3:
HIT THE INTERNET

What's going to separate you from other candidates is that you're not going to waste your time trying to prepare for everything (which is impossible), you're going to prepare for the *right* things. And how are you going to do that? With some good old-fashioned internet creeping.

On the company's website, look at sections with titles like "About Us" or "Careers." You'll probably see a selection of corporate photos and words like "Connection," "Community," "Give Us Your Firstborn," and so on. If you're a little weirded out, you're on the right page.

What you're looking for are common things the company talks about in terms of their values. What do they care about a lot? Typically, it's things like:

- Driving a better tomorrow for customers
- Changing the way the world does XYZ
- Building community/investing in communities
- Powering diversity, equity, and inclusion
- Redefining innovation

Take a shot every time you see one of these buzzwords and you'll black out. So maybe don't. If you do, wait until you sober up, and then write down the common topics defined in the company values and pick a couple you don't hate so you can drop them into your answers in the interview. For bonus points, you can even incorporate them into the introduction you prepared in step 2.

Then you're going to check out the description in the job posting and do the same thing. Look at what's listed in the requirements section and the qualifications. This is a cheat sheet. It's show and tell: They're literally telling you what they want to see, so show them. Write down the core qualifications and requirements listed on the posting and make a mental note: That's the stuff that matters.

STEP 4: ANTICIPATE QUESTIONS

Based on the list of skills and values you compiled in step 3, you can anticipate what questions the interviewer is going to ask. These questions may not be immediately obvious to you, but as a recruiter, I've been there, done that, so here are a few common questions you can expect to be asked about a given skill or value.

SKILL/ VALUE	POTENTIAL INTERVIEW QUESTIONS
Innovation	• Tell me about a time you developed and delivered an innovative solution. How did you generate buy-in? What was the result? • How do you define innovation in the work that you do? How do you innovate day to day?
Collaboration	• Tell me about a time you worked on a large team for a complex project. • What role do you tend to take on when you work on teams? • How do you encourage healthy collaboration at work?
Conflict Management	• Tell me about a time you encountered conflict at work. How did you navigate this? • How would you deal with getting pushback or negative feedback at work?
DEI	• How do you ensure your strategies incorporate diversity, equity, and inclusion? • How do you measure the success of DEI efforts?
Technical Skills	• How would you do [software engineering task]? • What does [data analytics term] mean?

SKILL/ VALUE	POTENTIAL INTERVIEW QUESTIONS
Leadership	• Tell me about a time you took on a position of leadership. • As a leader, how do you keep your team motivated through challenging quarters? • How do you manage performance and feedback if a member of your team is struggling?
Time Management	• How do you navigate having multiple competing priorities? • How do you structure your workday?
Stress Management	• How do you maintain balance during busy seasons? • How do you navigate stress at work?

If there's a value or skill I didn't cover and you're stumped about what the interviewer might ask, you can ask Google or AI to tell you what interview questions to use to assess for that value or skill.

STEP 5: HIGHLIGHT YOUR EXPERIENCE

Now it's time to actually prepare your interview answers. Did you just throw this book at the wall in frustration, sigh, and then pick it up again? Good. Get it out of your system. Because now you're ready to hear that you don't need to be prepared to answer every single one of these questions. It's impossible to be perfectly prepared to answer every single interview question, and the goal isn't to be perfectly rehearsed. You can't predict everything you'll be asked. The goal is to be prepared to highlight your experience, no matter the question.

You just need to be prepared with an example that comes to mind for the core skills and values listed. Basically, fill this in:

SKILL/ VALUE	EXAMPLE OF EXPERIENCE
Innovation	Working on a creative solution to team members' scheduling conflicts when I worked in retail. We developed a rotation of on-call employees to help out when people needed shifts covered. This was brand-new for the company and successfully reduced churn.
Collaboration	Working with a team of five other students on a group project for my business course. This included creating a safe space to brainstorm, delegating tasks, tracking deliverables, and providing feedback.
(Fill in your own value.)	(Fill in your own experience.)

STEP 6: BE A STAR

Maybe you've heard of the STAR method, possibly from a video of me popping up on your phone and saying, "Let me tell you about the STAR method!" I think it's incredible. The STAR method is a format of answering interview questions that essentially guarantees you won't say too much or too little. Remember, everyone has little to no attention span these days, so this really helps. This framework for answering questions can act as a guide when you're asked experience-based interview questions.

STAR stands for:

- Situation: 1 or 2 sentences to define the situation

- Task: 1 or 2 sentences to define what was required or what the problem was
- Action: 1 or 2 sentences to define your specific actions
- Result: 1 sentence to describe the results or outcome

For example, if an interviewer says, "Tell me about a time you managed conflict with a team member," a STAR-method answer might look like this:

- Situation: When I was working at a big tech company as a product manager, we had a product release that the marketing team wanted to launch ASAP, but the engineering team was concerned about their ability to deliver on time. This caused some tension on the team, and we had some conflict and confusion about the timeline.
- Task: We needed to define when the product would release and ensure both marketing and engineering were on board.
- Action: I booked working sessions with the marketing lead and engineering lead to present the pros and cons of both an early and a later release, and opened the floor for discussion. I facilitated the conversation so both teams felt heard, focusing on all parties and brainstorming potential solutions that balanced risk.
- Result: We landed on doing a later rollout to prevent the product from crashing. Having this open discussion with both teams helped the marketing team see the perspective of the engineering team, and when the

product launched, we had super positive feedback and no bugs or crashes.

Now it's your turn. Try using the STAR method to discuss the experiences you listed in step 5.

The reason this framework is so powerful is that in moments of panic, you can take a breath, root yourself in the STAR framework, and then start with S. All you need to do is pick which example to share, start describing the situation, and then follow the rest of the framework. Structures like this give you a life raft to hang on to when you feel like you may be drowning in nerves.

STEP 7:
GET HYPOTHETICAL

Alas, not every interview question is asking about your experience. There is also the dreaded hypothetical question. Yes, every good recruiter knows that you get the most valuable insights when you ask people about things they have actually done rather than about things they may or may not do in a made-up scenario. That doesn't stop some recruiters from asking. So if you're being asked a question that starts "What would you do if . . . ," here's a good structure to follow:

I would start by ________________________ because ________________. I would then ______________.

The rule of thumb is __________________________.

Here's an example.

QUESTION: What would you do in a scenario where both Zac Efron and Michael B. Jordan were fighting for your attention?

> ANSWER: *I would start by making sure each person was being given respect and understanding, because the goal is to ensure both men feel valued and heard. I would then get to know both of them to understand their motivation for pursuing me. The rule of thumb for me is to make sure I am making decisions that are data-backed and equitable.*

OK, I just needed to get that one out of my system. Here's a more realistic example.

> QUESTION: What would you do if you had a conflict with a coworker?
>
> ANSWER: *I would start by speaking directly with everyone involved, because it's important to understand where each party is coming from and make sure they feel heard. I would then work directly with my coworker to find common ground and work toward a solution. But every scenario is different, so if we needed to get outside perspective or ask for help, there's no shame in that. The rule of thumb for me is to operate with empathy and be open-minded about solutions, and that has always led me to healthy working relationships.*

Basically, tell the interviewer what you would do, why you'd do it, and what your general philosophy is with the topic at hand. You can't go wrong.

STEP 8: INTERVIEW THEM BACK

When a recruiter, hiring manager, or other team member is interviewing you, you're meant to be interviewing them back. It doesn't matter how bad the job market is or how sure you are that you're going to take this job if you get it; you should still be fully aware of the kind of company you're walking into. And part of that knowledge comes from asking the right questions in the interview.

If you don't ask questions at the end of an interview, you're doing yourself a massive disservice. Not only can you miss out on red flags about the organization, but you're also giving the interviewer the impression that you aren't that interested in the job. Asking two or three questions at the end of an interview sends a signal to the interviewer that you're genuinely interested in the position, hungry to learn, and smart enough to prepare for the interview.

Just don't ask things that are easily googleable, you know? Examples of questions *not* to ask include: What does this company do? How do you make money? Who are your competitors? How soon will I get promoted or get a raise?

Instead, try asking these:

- What are some of the proudest wins the team has had recently?
- What do you find separates a good employee from an exceptional one at this company?
- What has been a big challenge the team overcame recently?
- What does career growth and performance management look like?
- What technology and systems do the team use?
- What is the company's stance on remote and hybrid work?
- Do you have any reservations about me as a candidate?

(This one is only good if you're confident you did well, because it gives you one more chance to share more information and put to bed any concerns they may have.)

STEP 9: PRACTICE

If interviewing is a muscle you can grow, you need to put in the work to see the results. You're halfway there by preparing steps 1 through 7. But it's time for you to actually practice out loud.

With the list of skills and values you've identified, make up some interview questions and then record yourself answering them on your phone. You're going to hate this, because there's nothing worse than watching yourself back on camera (trust me). However, this is the hack that has helped my clients improve their interview skills, fast. Answer at least three questions, and then watch yourself back to notice:

- Are you using too many filler words (*like, um, you know*)?
- Are you speaking too fast or too slowly?
- Is your body language confident?
- Do you have any nervous habits? (I play with my hair when I'm stressed.)
- How do you react when you don't know the answer to a question?

Bringing awareness to the things that aren't helping you tell meaningful stories in interviews is 80 percent of the work in correcting it. Remember, you don't need to be perfect, you just need to be having a conversation about the thing you know best: yourself and your experience.

When you finish, take a five-minute break, then try again with a new set of questions. Rinse and repeat. I promise, soon you'll catch your naughty habits before they start.

STEP 10: DON'T PANIC

"I know what I need to say, but when they ask me . . . I freeze up."

"The second I'm asked a question I don't know the answer to, I panic."

"I overthink every single answer and then feel like I'm freaking out."

Even with all this preparation, you might be feeling like you're going to screw it up. Just so you know, this is an incredibly common feeling. You aren't a bad interviewer, so stop telling yourself that. The more you talk shit about yourself, the more you believe it. Instead, remind yourself that you're practicing and actually training yourself to be a great interviewer.

The reason most people feel stuck when they're asked challenging interview questions is that they feel they don't have the "right answer" to the question. In reality, they don't have the right mindset. There is no such thing as a perfect answer. You don't need to be perfect, you just need to be talking. Shift your focus from saying the *right* thing to saying *something*.

The next time you get hit with a wave of panic in an interview, this is what you're going to do:

1. Take one slow, deep breath.

2. Think of an example that aligns with the question, and if you don't have one, it's OK to answer the question hypothetically.

3. Pick the framework that aligns best with the questions (STAR or hypothetical).

4. Start by answering the first part of the framework, and the rest will follow. (Hack: Print out the frameworks and put them in your notebook or have them open on a tab on your laptop to reference.)

5. Buy yourself time if you need to—but save this for emergencies only. ("Sorry, the internet broke up. Can you please repeat yourself?" "Can I bug you to repeat the question?" "That's a great question—I may just need a moment!")

6. Talk before you think. Your thoughts don't need to be perfect or entirely hashed out. You just need to have a conversation. Pretend you're speaking to a friend about your experience. This is a conversation, not an interrogation.

Talking before thinking isn't the right advice for everyone, because some people seriously need to STFU. If you're reading this, though, you're self-aware enough to be investing in your career and communication skills. You're probably self-aware to a fault. You don't need to STFU. So how are you meant to start talking before you think? The answer is: Trust yourself. Trust that you can carry a conversation, and that even if the interview isn't "perfect," it'll still be good. Trust that you are worthy of the opportunities in front of you. You are incredible. Start acting like it.

INTERVIEW ETIQUETTE

I hope you took that pep talk to heart. Now, back to building your glutes—I mean, interview muscles. Speaking of ass, don't be one.

Here's a non-exhaustive list of things you should never do or say in interviews:

- Don't be late. And I define "late" as anything shy of being five minutes early.
- Don't skip a shower. This sounds self-explanatory. Take it from me: It isn't.
- Don't cuss. (My bad.)
- Don't speak ill of your current employer, boss, or *anyone*, even if they deserve it. It reflects poorly on you.
- Don't ask questions you should have googled that expose your lack of research.
- Don't talk out of your ass if you don't know the answer.
- Don't use excessive corporate speak.

While you're at it, make sure you take the time to send a thank-you email after the interview. Skipping this is a big no-no. Is a thank-you email the reason you will or won't get the job? Of course not. But it's one more way to stand out, show your gratitude, and build a relationship with the recruiter, whether it's for this opportunity or another. As a recruiter, I've worked with dozens of candidates who, for one reason or another, were not a good fit for a particular role. But because they were so thoughtful over email and actually made an effort to build a relationship with me, I would put them forward for opportunities for years to come. They played the long game, and it paid off.

The thank-you email can be as simple as:

Hi [name],

Thank you so much for making the time to connect with me. I really enjoyed learning more about the role and the team.

I look forward to staying in touch with any updates.

Talk soon,
[your name]

It's generally a lot harder to ghost someone who follows up, so sending an email to check in won't hurt you. If you don't hear back in five business days, follow up. Then follow up every week until you hear back.

A good follow-up email is simple and short:

Hi [name],

I hope you're well! I wanted to circle back regarding our interview on [date]. Just wanted to see if there were any updates or items needed on my end.

Best,
[your name]

Unfortunately, if it's been three weeks with no response, consider yourself ghosted. Which brings me to the last thing I'll say about ass: Sometimes the recruiter is one.

YOU GET TO JUDGE THE RECRUITER, TOO

One reason candidates get so in their heads during the interview process is because they forget they have power, too. You've done all this preparation to impress the recruiter, but are they impressing *you*?

In this wildly competitive job market, it's true that employers get to be picky with who they hire and that most of the control is in their court. But remember, the job market isn't always like this, and even when it's an employer's market, it doesn't mean you don't have any say. Ultimately, you get to decide if you sign the job offer. I recognize that the luxury of being selective is an uncommon privilege, but reminding yourself that you do have the power of choice (even if it's only in theory) gives you a little bit of that power back.

Think of it like this: If you're going on dates with someone who is kind, respectful, and good-looking, that doesn't mean they're the only good partner left in the world. If you think they are, you're going to act accordingly. You'll be more likely to shrink your needs to fit theirs, more likely to cancel other plans to see them, more likely to give off a whiff of desperation. This is what we call a scarcity mindset: the idea that there isn't enough of a good thing to go around.

Don't get it twisted. Both with good dates and good jobs, there is a shortage. But there isn't a total drought. Operating with a scarcity mindset means you'll be more likely to act from a place of anxiety and panic, which can actually make it harder to attract the results you want. If you believe the truth—that although there may not be *many* good jobs, there are *some*—you'll reclaim your power and remove some of that anxiety. If your current circumstances mean you don't have the privilege of being picky, that's OK. Just making the mental shift to know that you're allowed to pass judgment on the employer (even if you have no choice but to accept the job) can be enough.

All that to say, don't be scared to evaluate the interviewer right back. An interviewer who makes you feel like a burden or uncomfortable in any capacity is the ultimate red flag. The person you're meeting with is acting as the representative of the company, so if they have bad vibes, you can assume the apple doesn't fall far from the tree. Again, it doesn't mean you have to decline the job offer, it just means you're not going in blind.

My rule of thumb? If the interviewer is smug, dismissive, or straight-up rude at any stage in the process . . . run. They're showing you exactly how the company plans to treat you, and it doesn't look good.

This is especially true if they ghost you. All that time applying for jobs, networking, and interviewing, just to hear crickets from the recruiter? Discouraging is an understatement.

There is no silver bullet or one reason that companies ghost, but I've seen enough to tell you that it is *never* a reflection of you as a candidate. Sometimes recruiters manually track candidates, and unfortunately, people get missed through human error. Sometimes a recruiter gets taken off of an account and the candidate gets lost in transition. I've also seen recruiters who are just bad and don't think they need to decline a candidate.

Ultimately, preparing for interviews is exhausting and feels like a full-time job itself. I get it. But when you practice being a great interviewer, you're learning more than just how to schmooze recruiters to get the job you want. You're learning how to confidently communicate and advocate for yourself, and that's a muscle you'll flex for the rest of your career. Yes, you'll experience rejection and even ghosting—but we'll talk more about how to cope in the next chapter.

CHAPTER 7

ACT LIKE IT

Even the best career advice in the world isn't going to help you if you don't have the right attitude. You can do all the right things—define your career path, apply for all the right jobs, network like your life depends on it—and still not get the results you want. The reason? You're not acting like you deserve them. This chapter is dedicated to helping you show up with the confidence, attitude, and presence that will help you attract the opportunities you want.

You want to kick corporate ass? Act like it.

DEALING WITH REJECTION

I wish I was the kind of girl who could sit here and tell you that rejection is beautiful, the same way that my aunt told me I was beautiful in grade 4 when I had braces and headgear. Necessary? Yes. Beautiful? The jury is still out.

Guess what. Rejection fucking sucks. It feels like someone is telling you that you're not good enough, and it seems to confirm all the worst fears you have about yourself. And with financial pressures on top of that, it's a very heavy burden to carry. So let rejection hurt. Give yourself permission to mourn a little. But the truth is you're going to be told "no" more times than you're going to be told "yes." If you crumble every time you get rejected, the job search is going to hurt like hell. So have a cry if you need to, but then remind yourself of two things: (1) Rejection is not a reflection of your worth, and (2) rejection is redirection.

REJECTION IS NOT A REFLECTION OF YOUR WORTH

At one point in my career, I was rejecting over two thousand people a week—and that was just requests for first dates on dating apps. (Kidding.) But of those thousands of rejections I sent out, here's approximately how the numbers broke down:

- 50 percent of the time, candidates who got rejected were objectively really good candidates, but we were already further along in the process with other candidates before we saw their profiles
- 20 percent of the time, the candidate was really good, but other candidates had a slight upper hand due to niche desired experience or better connections and networking
- 20 percent of the time, the candidate simply wasn't qualified
- 10 percent of the time, the job got canceled or the budget was taken away, so the job itself no longer existed

Notice a pattern? Most of the rejections have nothing to do with a candidate not being a strong one. The rejections are entirely situational. In your case, someone else's referral got there first, the role got canned, or maybe you were a close second. I get it. Being a close second doesn't pay the bills. But it does mean nothing is wrong with you, and you do not have to doubt your worth as an employee or as a person.

REJECTION IS REDIRECTION

I do fundamentally believe that sometimes you're rejected from the job you *thought* was your dream because something much better is coming. That won't feel true until you've actually landed in the "something better," but one day, all the rejection will be part of your success story.

When I was in my early twenties, I applied for my *dream job* leading a large finance company's early-career recruitment function across the entire country. When I found out I got an interview, I was elated and spent hours practicing all my answers. In the interview itself, I was on fire, answering questions and being personable with the hiring manager.

And then at the end of the conversation, the hiring manager looked at me and said that she thought I was fantastic but that I was too junior for this role in particular.

I was crushed. I felt so ready for that position. They saw how many years of experience I had listed on my résumé. If I was "too junior," why did they even bring me in to interview in the first place? But I thanked her for her time and took a long, sad Uber ride home.

I had a good cry (in private) and complained to my mom. And then I sent the smartest email I have ever sent in my life. I wrote to the hiring manager who had rejected me and said, "Thank you so much for taking the time to interview me this week. I really enjoyed learning more about the role, and I so appreciate your feedback and honesty in the process. My goal is to continue growing my career, and I would love to know if you have any feedback for me or if you see any areas where I could improve?"

She replied. She told me I needed to work on leveraging data in my storytelling and that my experience lacked international impact.

So for the next six months, I went to my boss at the bank where I was working at the time and asked for more exposure internationally. She was incredible and put me on several high-visibility projects that helped me understand what I was missing. And you know what? That hiring manager was right. I wasn't ready for that job yet. I had more learning to do.

Six months later, when I applied for a senior recruiter role at a large tech company, I felt infinitely more prepared. And it showed, because not only did I get the gig, I literally doubled my earnings. Thank God I didn't get that first job, because something even better was around the corner.

Of course, this isn't the case all the time. Sometimes rejection is just rejection. The honest truth is that no advice I can give you will make rejection feel better or relieve the pressure of a long, painful job hunt when there are bills to pay and mouths to feed. But I can tell you that there will be a light at the end of the tunnel, even if that tunnel is long and dark.

IF YOU FEEL COMFORTABLE, ASK ABOUT IT

One of the best ways to move past the pain of rejection is to feel like you're in control of the situation as much as possible. Asking for feedback is an incredible way to feel like you're in the driver's seat, while also making the space to learn and level up. When you get rejected from an opportunity, consider reaching out and asking for feedback over email.

Is everyone going to reply with honest and valuable critique? Of course not. But all it takes is one person to give you insight into why you weren't the candidate they selected. That information, if used to inform your development plan, can accelerate your career in ways you never imagined. You can use that feedback as a chance to learn. That's what I did, and it changed my career.

Now, as a white, cis woman, I knew there would be little to no chance of repercussions when I asked for this feedback. I wasn't labeled as needy, aggressive, or resistant, and when I asked my then boss for more international opportunity, she interpreted it in a positive way. But not everyone has as much privilege as I do. So does this advice work? Yes, but the realities of overt and covert discrimination can significantly impact how effective and safe the advice may be, given each person's specific situation. So, as always, take what resonates and leave what doesn't.

LISTENING TO FEEDBACK

Speaking of asking for feedback, this is another area where you'll need to learn to operate with the right attitude. Because getting feedback sucks! But maturing is realizing that feedback is a gift, as long as the sender isn't an asshole. A boss or peer who's constantly picking you apart isn't giving you feedback, they're being a bully (which we'll talk about in chapter 11). But someone who's delivering feedback in an empathetic way with the intention to see you grow is someone you should value deeply. You'll never grow if you're surrounded by people who tell you everything you do is perfect—or if your highest priority is protecting your ego.

Getting feedback either in the interview process or over the course of your career is inevitable. Feeling like it's a personal attack isn't.

If feedback about your career feels personal, it's probably because your identity is too tied to your work. Criticism about your work is about the things you do, not who you are. If you can't separate the two yet, reread chapter 2. You'll get there.

Anyone who says they like getting feedback is a liar. No one likes it. But here's how to not be a dick about it.

1. Don't get defensive. This isn't an attack. This is feedback on a task you've completed, or job you've applied to, not on who you are as a person. Don't try to overexplain or justify yourself.

2. Take a breath. Really listen. Understand that the person who's sharing this is doing it because they see your potential and care about you.

3. The first thing out of your mouth should be "Thank you," even if you don't mean it. Thank them for the feedback and for their honesty.

4. Actually implement the change. This is a chance to get better. Maybe this means you identify mentors to help you grow a specific skill, ask to take on new work, take an online course, or simply learn new skills on YouTube. If nothing else, getting better means you get paid more.

Whether you're getting feedback after an interview process or at another point in your career, be growth-minded (even if you're faking it at first). It will make you feel more in control of the outcome and put a positive spin on an otherwise draining situation.

IMPOSTOR SYNDROME

Have you heard of impostor syndrome? It's that dreadful, nagging voice in the back of your head telling you:

- You're underqualified.

- You've only gotten to where you are because of luck.
- You're likely going to fail.
- You're a fraud.
- You don't actually know what you're doing.
- Everyone around you is smarter, has more experience, and makes fewer mistakes than you.
- Soon, everyone around you will realize you don't belong here.

Nearly 70 percent of adults experience impostor syndrome at least once in their lifetime, including 75 percent of women in executive leadership positions. Yes, all of these folks with fancy degrees and C-suite jobs still feel like frauds. The people you find intimidating have all the same doubts and worries as you; you just don't have access to their internal monologue.

Many people think that once they land their ideal job or get to a certain salary, they won't feel like a fraud anymore. Instead, once they make it to one goal, they set a new one, and the cycle continues. The bar is raised, and so is the self-doubt.

Living with impostor syndrome is not just emotionally taxing. It also directly impacts how likely someone is to raise their hand for opportunities, ask for raises, or apply for jobs. After all, you're only going to ask for the opportunities you think you deserve. In short, impostor syndrome can keep you miserable and underpaid.

Unsurprisingly, rates of reported impostor syndrome skyrocket for women, BIPOC folks, and LGBTQ+ folks, largely due to lack of representation and systemic barriers. For people who are marginalized in some way, the feeling that you don't belong in certain rooms is often reinforced by microaggressions and a lack of equal access to opportunity.

Knowing that, how can you defeat impostor syndrome? Here are a few tips.

1. **Keep an ongoing list of your career accolades.** I call this my "I Did That" list. It tracks every single win in your career, no matter how small, and any positive feedback you receive, either verbally or in writing. Taking time to reflect on your career wins will deepen the neural pathways for positive reinforcement, and in moments of self-doubt, instead of wallowing in the fear that you aren't enough, you can review this list. It's pretty hard to tell yourself you're a loser when there are pages of data proving you're not.

2. **Find a mentor.** Having a mentor, in my experience, can significantly reduce impostor syndrome. And it's not just because it sounds cool and sexy to say, "I was talking to my mentor, and . . ." It's because having regular check-ins with your mentor can help validate your decisions, provide feedback, and hype you up. That said, if you're a woman, BIPOC, LGBTQ+, or part of any other group that's underrepresented in leadership positions, it can make finding mentors with shared experiences more challenging. In that case, employee resource groups, professional associations, and conferences can be wonderful resources for identifying mentors with a variety of lived experiences.

3. **Challenge your binary thinking.** Isn't it interesting how when you make a mistake or fail, it's all your fault, but when you succeed, it isn't all to your credit? Start noticing moments where you internalize mistakes and

externalize accomplishments. Ask yourself: "If my best friend were sharing the same story, would I react the same way?" Having a mentor who has similar experiences to yours or has overcome similar feelings is perfect for these situations because it lets you talk through these concerns with someone who's been there. Impostor syndrome can't thrive when you challenge this binary mindset, because it means you aren't a faker hiding among perfectly successful people; we're all imperfect.

These lifestyle and mindset changes will help you combat impostor syndrome and rewire your brain to be more self-assured. In the meantime, you'll need to fake it until you make it.

FAKE IT TILL YOU MAKE IT

You've probably been told to "fake it till you make it" before a big test, interview, or date, or by me one sentence ago. The point is to encourage you to act like you're confident even when you're not. The phrase is thrown around so much that in some ways it's starting to lose its power. But it's not just a cliché; it's science.

Your brain actively reviews your physical actions to determine how you're feeling, which is why forcing a smile when you're having an awful day can actually make you feel better. Yes, acting like a happy person actually makes you happier. How crazy is that? "Fake it till you make it" can also be explained by self-perception theory, which describes the human tendency to understand our feelings and attitudes by observing what we're actually doing. Essentially, when you act confident (even if you aren't), over time, you'll begin to see your actions through the lens of a confident person. Slowly, it will no longer feel like you're "acting like" a confident person but, rather, like you *are* a confident person.

Why does this feel so uncomfortable? It requires you to muscle through impostor syndrome and start acting like you're worthy before you feel like you are. It asks you to act like your ideal self before you even become that person. It forces you to rewire your thinking from "Why would they pick me?" to "Why *wouldn't* they pick me?"

To be clear, "faking it" doesn't mean being obnoxious, entitled, showy, or arrogant. It's not about acting like some caricature of a confident person. It's about showing up as the most confident, successful, and self-assured version of *you*. It is not a character you're playing, it's an intention you're setting that is unique to you.

Who Are You, Ideally?

In a notebook or journal, answer the questions below through the lens of your ideal future self. The more specific you get, the better.

- *What values matter most to you? What boundaries do you set to reinforce them?*
- *Who do you spend most of your time with? How would you describe those people? What qualities do they have? How do they make you feel about yourself?*
- *What is your outlook on the world around you? How open are you to new people or experiences?*
- *How do you define success? What would a successful life truly look like?*
- *How do you interact with people around you, both professionally and personally?*
- *How do you receive and deliver feedback? How much of your self-concept comes from within you and how much comes from what the world tells you?*

- *How do you ask for the things you want?*
- *How do you handle fear or anxiety, especially in the context of work?*
- *How do you stand up for yourself when people are trying to cross your boundaries or manipulate you?*
- *How do you operate in group settings?*
- *How do you make others feel about themselves?*

This list should give you a rough outline of how your ideal self shows up in the world. And if this is your ideal self, act like it. Before you attend an interview, networking conversation, or workday, ground yourself in what you've written down. How would the ideal version of you present themself in this situation? How would they navigate nerves or anxiety? How would they be a self-advocate? Draw awareness to how your ideal self would tackle your day, and channel that.

But remember, faking it only works if you're embodying the best version of yourself. Otherwise, you're just . . . fake. Staying grounded in who your ideal self is and baking in these hacks will help you accelerate your career and fast-track your confidence journey.

CONFIDENT COMMUNICATION 101

Folks who exhibit confident behaviors are more likely to get leadership roles and access to new opportunities, largely because they *act like* they can handle it, and people believe them. I've seen this thousands of times in my coaching, but also in my own career. When I first moved into recruiting, I was nineteen years old with absolutely zero experience. I didn't know how to send a calendar hold or write a professional email. But without fail, opportunities continued to fall into my lap. I was asked to present at a large internal town hall, nominated for promotions, and so on, not because I had the experience or skill, but because I acted like I did.

When I was complimented at work, I didn't deflect and minimize my accomplishments. I would simply say, "Thank you." When I was handed new tasks, I would say, "Anything I don't know how to do, I'll figure out"—and then I did. I said yes as much as humanly possible to new projects, opportunities, and events. I talked the talk so well that eventually I learned how to walk the walk.

We all have the ability to figure shit out and learn on the go. But to access it, you need to have the confidence that you're capable, which is the exact opposite of what your impostor syndrome wants you to believe. Operating with confidence (even if you're faking it) is going to open doors for you at every stage in your career. So in the context of careers, how does a confident person communicate?

Here's the thing: The message you're sending to the world is very rarely what you're saying with your words. Words actually account for only about 7 percent of the message; tone of voice is 38 percent, and body language is a whopping 55 percent. So as you sit in an interview hung up on trying to say the "right thing," realize that *what* you say matters much less than *how* you say it.

IMPROV THEORY

Confidence isn't about knowing you'll say or do the perfect thing, it's trusting that no matter what, you'll figure it out—and it's about leveraging your words, tone, and body language accordingly. It's trusting that even if you stumble in an interview, you'll bounce back, because you know your shit. Unbeknownst to most confident people out there, the reason they communicate so freely is because they're using techniques from something called improv theory.

Many people don't know this about me, but my first major in university was actually theater. I won't bore you with the details, but

I survived two days of classes before I switched my major to business. For a long time, that made me feel like a failure, but in hindsight, I can see how my passion for theater was foundational to my career, even though I didn't end up pursuing it professionally. It made me a strong storyteller and a strong writer, and above all, it exposed me to improv.

Improv, short for improvisation, is a popular style of live acting where the plot, characters, and dialogue are all determined live in the moment onstage. You'll often see improv actors asking the crowd to shout out locations or scenes for the actors to use onstage. Beyond being very funny, it's remarkable that a group of actors can create an entire storyline on the spot. The best skill I've ever been taught in my life is the ability to think on my feet, which I can directly attribute to my connection to improv.

So how *do* they do it? Well, they operate with a few core principles in mind:

1. **"Yes, and":** In improv theater, you're never supposed to shut down someone else's improvised idea by saying no or responding in a scene-ending way, no matter how obscure the scene. Instead, you receive what the other person is saying and build on it. If someone says, "I'm a banana," you don't say, "No, you're not, bananas can't talk." You say, "Yes, and I'm a monkey." It's really the art of just going with it.

2. **Active listening:** Improv acting only works when each character is genuinely paying attention to what the other is saying so they can react appropriately. Actors recognize that listening to what's happening is just as important to the scene as speaking.

3. **Embrace mistakes:** Mistakes onstage like fumbling over a word or mispronouncing something doesn't stop the

entire scene. Improv actors can't ask for permission to start over. They embrace the mistake and keep rolling—which often makes the scene even funnier.

4. Be a little crazy: The only way improv theater works is when the actors commit to the bit so hard that the audience believes the (completely ridiculous) story they're telling. And the only way actors can do that is to, frankly, not give a shit and to kill their fear of being judged in the pursuit of creating enjoyable theater.

Improv theory is a method of communication that pulls from these core pillars of improvisational theater. In essence, it's a communication philosophy that encourages quick thinking and rolling with the punches. When you observe folks who act confident, you'll notice they exhibit the same behaviors. This is especially helpful in interviews or corporate settings, because your ability to carry a conversation, be flexible, and adapt is something that will help you stand out.

Let's take a look at how you would apply the improv principles above to inject confidence into your daily communication.

1. "Yes, and": Actively practice receiving the information the other person is sharing and building on it, even if your response isn't "perfect." If you're asked challenging questions in interviews, don't shut down and say you don't know the answer. Instead, think about how you can build on the conversation to keep it flowing and try sharing how you would go about finding that answer. If you're networking with an executive and they share something interesting about their career, follow up and ask more questions based on the information they're giving you. This isn't a solo show; you're meant to cocreate something with the other person. Accept the

information being presented and make your immediate next step to build on it.

2. Active listening: Where many people trip up in corporate conversations is they put so much emphasis on trying to say the perfect thing that they often aren't listening to understand—they're listening just long enough until it's their turn to speak. Amazing conversationalists are amazing listeners. They are curious about and interested in the information being shared with them. Especially in the case of interviews or negotiations: Remember these are conversations, not interrogations. The spotlight isn't on only you. Give yourself permission to ask questions and express interest in what the other person is saying. It can alleviate so much pressure and make the conversation feel much more enjoyable.

3. Embrace mistakes: Expect that you'll make mistakes, both in interviews and at work. You'll say the "wrong" thing and not know the answer to every question. That's all totally natural. You don't need to be perfect or have all the right answers to be the person who gets the opportunity. Learn to embrace these mistakes as part of the scene, because you can't close the curtains every time you trip up. Like improv actors onstage, take a quick breath to recenter yourself, don't catastrophize, and go on with the show.

4. Be a little crazy: Start to accept the worst-case scenario. Let's say you bombed that interview and didn't get the job. That doesn't mean you aren't a qualified candidate with a bright future ahead of you, it just means this wasn't the job you were meant to get. Give yourself

permission to detach from the outcome, and the outcome will get better.

All of this is much easier in theory than it is in practice. Which brings me to a very critical point: You need to *practice.* Few people are born great communicators. It's a skill that is rehearsed until it feels natural. Faked until it's real. I know you're probably cringing at this, not wanting to talk to yourself any more than this book has already forced you to, but the reality is that without active practice to rewire your behaviors, nothing is going to change.

Improv Exercises

If you struggle with confident communication, I highly recommend joining an improv class, even if it's only once or twice. But if that's not something you're comfortable with or ultimately just sounds bad, here are some alternatives to help you beef up your conversational skills, especially in the context of interviews.

1. *Ask a friend to play charades or another improvisational game with you to help you practice operating with these core principles in mind.*

2. *Ask AI to ask you ten random questions and only give yourself one minute to answer each. The subjects should be completely random like "Explain why pizza is better than pasta" or "Talk to me about your favorite TV show of all time." Then record yourself answering each question following the improv principles above.*

3. *Do a DIY TED Talk. Select a random topic that you're familiar with (this may be a book you like, a sport you*

follow, etc.) and record yourself delivering a sixty-second speech on the subject. Let it feel silly, let there be mistakes. And then watch the recording to learn where you can improve next time.

ELIMINATING FILLER WORDS

In addition to bringing improv theory into your conversations, it's important to become aware of some of the bad communication habits many of us have. I'm looking at you, filler words. Filler words like *like, you know,* and *um* can easily creep into both conversations and presentations, making you look less confident and professional in corporate settings. You'll probably notice them when you play back your DIY TED talk, cringing.

We tend to use filler words when we're nervous, to buy time for thinking (and overthinking). Most people aren't aware of how many they're using in conversation, which is why awareness is half the battle.

Practicing improv will naturally reduce your use of filler words by improving your ability to be more present in these moments. You can also record yourself doing speaking exercises like the one in the previous section to clock how many times you use filler words and practice using them less. Unless you're actually giving a TED talk, you don't need to eliminate them completely, but the fewer you use, the more confident you'll sound in your next big meeting.

TONE OF VOICE

Your tone of voice during interviews, presentations, and networking can play a massive role in how confident and competent people perceive you to be. I do want to note that perception isn't reality, and many of the communication styles that are rewarded at work are not inclusive for all neurodivergent folks. This needs to change, but until it does, I want to offer ways to work around it and through it. One of the biggest tips is to use different inflections, pauses, and pacing in your voice, when possible, to add to your storytelling.

Don't feel the need to rush through your words so quickly that it's hard to follow. Confident people are comfortable slowing down and taking up space to deliver their message, because they believe their message is worth hearing. However slow you think you're speaking, take it a notch slower.

If you're struggling with this, watch a few keynote speeches on YouTube and write down which ones felt the most engaging. What tone, cadence, and energy did the presenter bring? How can you mirror that?

BODY LANGUAGE

Have you ever been at a party and watched someone walk into the venue and immediately draw all eyes toward them? Those magnetic people who seem to attract positive attention without even having to speak are people who've mastered the art of confident body language. In this highly competitive job market, oozing confidence is going to get you noticed.

Strong body language in the context of careers includes:

- Sitting up or standing tall with a strong posture
- Open body language: not crossing your arms and keeping your shoulders and back open
- Making eye contact if that's feasible for you
- Smiling when delivering messages (but, like, not in a creepy way)

- Talking with your hands, leaning in, and taking up space when speaking
- Not fidgeting, playing with your hair, etc.
- Not being glued to your phone

Remember, using the body language of a confident person will eventually help trick you into becoming confident yourself.

BRINGING IT ALL TOGETHER

From deciding to fake it till you make it to using improv theory to boost your communication, the theme of this chapter is really *acting*. (See, Mom, I told you the theater classes would pay off!) Beef up your acting chops and defeat impostor syndrome by actively practicing the art of going with the flow and communicating confidently. Trust that the more you act like your ideal self, the more quickly you will become that person.

CHAPTER 8

DESIGN YOUR PERSONAL BRAND

Showing up with confidence gets you in the room, but making a lasting impression and having a defined sense of self keeps you there. So if the "faking it" is about acting right while shifting our thoughts and behaviors, the "making it" is about feeling authentically connected to the person we want to become.

That, my friends, is your personal brand. This chapter is going to help you define your personal brand for the modern world and teach you how to leverage it to get ahead.

I'm going to say something that might make you roll your eyes: *Your personal brand matters.*

I know that sounds like some old-school corporate BS, and depending on whose advice you're taking, you might be right. The old-school idea of personal branding is to formally define what your corporate identity is: What industry are you an expert in? What work are you known for?

On the surface, these are perfectly fine anchors to use for your personal brand, but they come with risk. The industry you work in, your areas of focus, and even your capacity for stress are all guaranteed to evolve over time, so tying your personal brand to external factors doesn't feel like the best long-term strategy. I'd argue the modern idea of personal brand should be defined very differently.

By my definition, your personal brand is what other people think of when they think of you. And once they've determined what your brand is, it's hard to change it. Getting it right the first time matters. Have you ever planned a night out with some friends and intentionally *not* invited one person because they have a track record of steamrolling the conversation and overdoing it on the prosecco? Or, conversely, have you ever booked a vacation around the availability of that one friend who's such a good time that the trip wouldn't be complete if they aren't in attendance? You know their personal brand and act accordingly. Your brand determines which doors will open for you and which will remain closed.

What makes for a solid personal brand in your career? The formula is simple:

> Confidence + being decent at your job + making others feel good = good personal brand

Essentially, if you act like you deserve to be there, do work that proves you deserve to be there, and make people *want* you to be there, you've nailed your personal brand.

HOW TO NOT SUCK AT YOUR JOB

We've already covered the confidence of it all, so let's crack into how to be good or at least decent at your job. You can be bursting with confidence, but if you suck at your job, it won't matter. Being a "personality hire"—someone who's hired because they're fun to be around, not because of their actual skills—will only get you so far, because eventually people will catch on to the fact that that's all you've got.

"Does Emily do anything? I never see her working."

"Emily hasn't made a sale in over a month."

"I reviewed the report Emily put together. It was a mess."

These are the kinds of comments your personal brand can't recover from. So make sure you're decent at what you do. Decent doesn't mean perfect. It means you have a high say:do ratio.

The say:do ratio is something I learned from a very successful talent acquisition leader I worked with. (Jen, if you're reading this, thank you.) It measures how much of what you *say* you're going to do actually gets *done*, well and on time. Every time you miss a deadline or submit a half-assed project, your ratio of what you say to what you do drops. Eventually, people lose trust in you and no longer believe you when you say you're on it.

Mastering your say:do ratio is actually pretty simple if you follow three key principles.

1. **Don't bite off more than you can chew.** If you have a habit of overcommitting and underdelivering, your say:do ratio will suffer. Be realistic with your workload. Yes, sometimes that means you need to say no to certain tasks, and it'll feel uncomfortable. But it'll be more uncomfortable if you don't deliver on your promises and start to be seen as incompetent. (I'll give you some workplace boundary hacks later in the chapter to help you say no without feeling like you're slacking.)

2. **Track your tasks.** Even if the task seems small, write down what you need to deliver on and by when. This will prevent you from forgetting anything or delivering late. Even if you hardly ever forget anything, I'm telling you, one day you will.

3. **Overcommunicate.** By the time someone must ask you for an update, they've already lost trust in you. Communicate where you are in the process, and if there

are hurdles or you need support, say so *early*. Go out of your way to provide status updates to relevant parties, more than you think is necessary.

Ace your say:do ratio, and the rest will follow.

MAKING OTHERS FEEL GOOD

If you're projecting confidence and you're sure people can rely on you at work, you're ready to refine the last element of your personal brand: how you make people feel. There's a quote often attributed to Maya Angelou: "People will forget what you said, people will forget what you did, but people will never forget how you made them feel." You can say all the right things in an interview and still leave a sour taste in the recruiter's mouth if you didn't make them *feel* good. This aligns with research showing that positive and negative emotions impact memory recall more than facts.

How Do I Make Other People Feel?

Answer the following questions in a notebook or in Google Docs.

1. *What do you generally want people to feel around you? For example, I would write:*
   - *Empowered and energized*
   - *Understood and validated in their feelings*
   - *Joyful, like they're having fun even if the task at hand isn't fun*
   - *Safe emotionally, without fear of judgment*

2. *How do you have to show up for that to be true? Here's mine:*

    - *Be a high-energy person who goes out of their way to compliment others and build them up*
    - *Be a very active listener*
    - *Give off happy energy, even in times of stress*
    - *Be open to new perspectives and don't lean into judgment*

3. *Now put it all together by filling in the blanks in this sentence: I want people to feel ________________ around me, so I act ______________________.*

My example: *I want people to feel empowered, validated, seen, confident, and energized around me, so I act empowering and validating toward others, energizing them and lifting them up.*

...

That's the final component of having a good personal brand: being a source of joy to the people around you.

In some ways, it's simple. But remember, this is how you conduct yourself in the everyday hellscape that is work. It's easier to be fun and happy when things aren't stressful. The true test of your character and brand is how you handle things when shit hits the fan. How would you respond to a coworker gossiping about you? Your boss delivering negative feedback in a bit of a bitchy way? Your director asking you to work overtime? If you want your personal brand to be about joy, validation, and empowerment, you need to be embodying that even in moments where you want to throw a phone at someone's head.

It may seem cheesy to sit and think about how you'll show up in difficult moments, but difficult moments will inevitably happen in any career. Running through these hypothetical situations will prepare you to act in a way that won't damage your reputation.

USING YOUR BRAND TO YOUR ADVANTAGE

I vividly remember a candidate—let's call him Roger—who was interviewing for a software engineering position. Roger's résumé was stacked, he had incredible experience, and he was the candidate I was most excited to present. In his interview with the hiring manager, he answered questions well. But afterward, the hiring manager called me to express concern about Roger's level of judgment. When asked about why certain product launches in his previous role were unsuccessful, he expressed negative sentiments about other members of his team. Objectively, he was correct. These people sounded like morons. But it gave my hiring manager some pause. Was Roger judgmental and negative in the face of conflict?

If Roger had clearly defined what his personal brand was, he may have delivered his message in a different way.

Your personal brand lives everywhere, both online and in person. Having a personal brand means:

- You have a consistent reputation, so people are more likely to approach you with new opportunities because they know what to expect.

- Your brand is working for you, even when you're not there. Your reputation precedes you, so there may be people speaking about your brand even when you're not there, opening up (or closing) opportunities for you.

- You'll likely get more grace when you do fuck up, because you have a track record of being good.

OH, TO BE LIKED AND SEEN

Have you noticed it's almost never the smartest or most qualified person who gets the job or the promotion? It's the most visible and the most well liked. If you have limited time to invest in your career, I would genuinely rather have you invest it in improving your likability and visibility rather than your actual intellect and skill.

Believe me, I know how fucked up that is. But the ugly truth is that meritocracy is a myth. People are not hired, paid, and promoted based on skill, talent, and hard work. Of course, those things can be *factors* in success, and they often are. But in a world built on racism, capitalism, sexism, and every other -ism, merit alone isn't going to grow your career.

A solid personal brand is going to attract the right jobs, promotions, and people into your life because it supercharges the two most important factors in career growth: visibility and likability.

LIKABILITY

Do people like you? Usually I'd say to hell with anyone's opinions, but in this case, that would make me a really bad friend, because how much people like you will change the course of your career.

Well-liked individuals are significantly more likely to receive career-advancing opportunities, have better relationships with their coworkers, and make more money. Now, I don't want you trying to shapeshift your entire personality to cater to the people around you. Rather, I want to help you highlight the great qualities that already exist within you and that align with your ideal self.

Based on science and my opinion (both equally credible), there are a few universal commonalities shared by likable people:

- They celebrate the wins of others out loud and share credit.

- They ask genuine questions about those around them.
- They speak highly of others, even when they're not there.
- They don't have big egos. They admit when they're wrong, aren't too proud to ask for help, and don't feel the need to boast.
- They're emotionally intelligent and can read the room.
- They remember things about those around them, like names and major life events.
- They thank people regularly.
- They're authentic and don't need to put on an act.
- They're inclusive and don't exhibit "mean girl" energy or behaviors.
- They're happy both in energy and in body language.

Again, you aren't here to change who you are. Instead, look at this list, decide what qualities come naturally to you, and mindfully lean into them. And if you see a few that you'd like to be better at, work on developing them.

VISIBILITY

You know that old saying "If a tree falls in a forest and no one is there to hear it, does it make a sound?" In the context of work, the answer is no. You can be doing the most high-value, complex, life-changing work in the entire world, and if no one knows what you're working on, it doesn't matter. You can be the best employee that company has ever seen, and if you're not highly visible, you'll be passed up for raises, promotions, and recognition over and over again.

Visibility at work means that key decision-makers and the people who matter know who you are, what you're working on, and your personal brand. But don't get it twisted. We don't give a shit if your rude coworker thinks poorly of you. They aren't the person who's making significant decisions about your career future. Let them dislike you. Instead, focus on being visible to your manager, leadership at the company, and teams you collaborate with. The goal here isn't to be a kiss-ass who begs for attention, it's simply to make sure you get recognized for the work you're already doing.

HACKING LIKABILITY AND VISIBILITY AT WORK

Being likable really just means that people find you enjoyable to work with because you aren't a dick. Being visible boils down to ensuring others understand what you're working on and see your value. Here's how to hack likability and visibility at work and create a fantastic personal brand.

LIKABILITY AND VISIBILITY WITH COWORKERS

There is a true science to being liked and visible at work, whether it's in office or virtually. As someone who has worked in HR for all of my career, I can tell you that the people who get ahead are the ones who are top of mind. Here is *exactly* what to do to stand out at work without being an annoying suck-up:

If you work remote:

- Be active-ish in work group chats by replying to people's messages and voting in polls. (But don't reply to *everything*, or people will think you have nothing else to do.)

- On Mondays, reach out to your team's group chat and ask how everyone's weekend was. On Fridays, wish everyone a happy Friday.

- Be the first to shout out members of your team for their help on something or great results in your group chat.

- Attend meetings on-camera as much as possible and look engaged (even if you're faking it, because realistically, everyone is).

- Reach out to people you haven't spoken to in a while over your work messenger to check in and see how they are. This is especially valuable if they're slightly more senior than you.

- With the support of your boss, reach out to interesting (and well-regarded) people to have a virtual coffee chat and learn more about their team. This is a surefire way to ensure more people know who you are and see you as a highly invested learner.

- Don't skip the pleasantries over email. Ask people how they are and follow up with them on life events they shared with you. This stuff goes a long way.

- Be a quick responder to messages and try to be online during working hours (even if you are, in fact, at the nail salon—just bring your laptop).

If you work in the office:

- At the start of every day, make a point to say good morning or a quick hi to everyone you walk by on your floor until you get to your desk. This helps people associate you with being confident, kind, and considerate.

- When you settle into your desk, don't skip the "Hi, how was your weekend?" with the team. But by about 9:15, you should be locked in to work, because there is a balance here. You don't want to be perceived as someone who chats all day.

- Be visible *working*. This doesn't mean you need to be the first in and the last to leave. But don't be the last in and the first to leave.

- Look busy. Take some meetings from your desk, type intensely, stare at your computer screen with intention. If there's nothing to do, girl, you better fake it.

- Attend the social events and have meaningful conversations while you're there (more on that to come).

- Play the Empty Coffee Cup Game. Pick up an empty coffee mug and walk to your floor's coffee machine. On the way, stop by two or three people's desks to check in and see how they are. The exchange should be less than four minutes—just ask how they're doing or how their weekend was, then say, "I'm about to fill up before a meeting, but see you soon." The coffee cup gives you the perfect excuse to spark a conversation and then leave it. Doing this one or two days a week will help you build casual relationships across the floor, and trust me, every relationship counts.

These hacks will make sure other people at the office know who you are and have a positive association with you. They'll let your boss and adjacent teams see you playing nice in the sandbox, but they'll also help you meet potential new mentors and, dare I say, friends.

LIKABILITY AND VISIBILITY WITH YOUR BOSS

Raise your hand if you've ever had a manager who truly had no clue what you were working on at any point in time. For the record, my hand is raised. How do these people know so little and get paid so much? I don't know. But I do know there are few things as detrimental for your career as a manager who doesn't know what you're working on.

Your manager is the ultimate gatekeeper of your growth at your organization. They're the person who is primarily responsible for any raises, promotions, or new opportunities presented to you. Even something as simple as getting the opportunity to work on a new project will typically need your manager's approval. In most cases, it isn't appropriate for you to reach out to senior leaders to flaunt your work or ask for something, so it's critical that your boss is advocating for you in rooms you're not in. We'll talk about how to handle toxic bosses soon, but assuming your manager is a relatively normal person who doesn't suck the life out of you, you can use likability and visibility to take them from being *your manager* to being *your advocate*.

It starts with making sure your boss generally likes you as a person. This is actually a lot easier than people realize. Take interest in them, be authentic, and be a go-getter. That's really it. Taking interest in your boss can be as simple as asking how they're doing and *meaning it*. This can also trickle into learning on the job. Take genuine interest in learning from your boss professionally, ask them questions, and compliment and thank them often. Ask them for their opinions, feedback, and perspective. This is going to make them feel validated and important. People love that.

Remember, being authentic means you aren't trying to be someone else—you're just trying to be the best version of yourself. You can do this by sharing your opinions, pushing back, and pitching new ideas when appropriate. It's much easier to like someone who has a defined sense of self and point of view than someone who's merely a yes-man. (There's nothing more annoying than that one coworker who says things like "I was just about to say that" in a meeting after someone else shares an original thought. Baby, if you were just about to say that, why didn't you?)

Finally, if you want your boss to like you, you can't operate with a victim mentality. This is a bit of a tough-love tip, but that's what I'm here for. There is nothing that will make you more disliked at work than constantly complaining and raising problems without solutions. Operating with the attitude that you can figure things out, can take initiative, and don't need your boss to hold your hand is something every leader desires. It doesn't mean you never raise questions or ask for help, it just means you make a valiant effort to figure things out on your own first. The art of FSO (figuring shit out) will get its own section later on.

It's also your job to make sure your manager understands what you're working on. It starts with your one-on-one meeting with your boss. In most roles, you'll have a formal catch-up meeting with your boss either weekly, biweekly, or monthly (and if you don't have one, ask to set one up). The value of these meetings is for your boss to share updates, offer live feedback, and of course, get a status update on your work. Remember, by the time someone has to ask for updates, you're too late.

In these conversations, be proactive and make a point to ask your boss, "Would it be helpful if I provide a quick update on where we're at?" Usually, they'll say yes. Then, without overexplaining or bragging, in less than three minutes, provide a summary of what you're working on, any positive results, and any blockers you need to flag. Doing this weekly is the best way for your boss to understand the value of your work and learn how you overcome any obstacles that they may not have known about.

This next strategy is bold, but it works. In your one-on-one meeting with your boss, ask if it would be helpful for you to provide weekly status updates via email because "I already track that for my own personal growth." They will likely say yes, and then, BOOM, you reference your "I Did That" list and send out a weekly email to your boss outlining the status of your work, with specific shout-outs of the things you did well and any positive feedback you got.

If just the thought of doing this makes you cringe, I get it. It's embarrassing. Unfortunately, work environments are embarrassing! This corny shit works, and sometimes we need to be uncomfortable to get what we want. If this feels super inorganic to your brand, you can instead send an email to your boss when there's a positive status update on something you're working on or positive feedback you've received from your peers or clients. You can say something along the lines of "Just sharing the below status update/feedback for your visibility" or "Sharing the below status update/feedback, as I'll be adding it to my performance tracker."

Again, if this feels super *pick me*, it is. I urge you to get over it. You can carry that discomfort all the way to the bank. Once the check clears, I think you'll feel just fine.

LIKABILITY AND VISIBILITY WITH OTHER LEADERS

It's critical for executives and senior leaders to know and like you, because usually they're the people who control budgets, which means they have a say in raises, new roles being created, and so on. They also have the power to invent opportunities for you and connect you to influential people internally. The hack to getting leaders to notice you (other than by relying on your manager) is to get involved in highly visible work. You need to be doing a *little* something extra to make sure leaders see you making an impact.

In my opinion, one of the best ways to do this is to join an employee resource group (ERG). These are essentially internal groups sponsored by your company to drive community engagement. Usually ERGs will host events, lunch-and-learns, and volunteering opportunities across the organization that executives *need* to attend. Joining an ERG is a great way to meet those executives—as well as network with people outside of your function at the company. I've actually met some of my closest friends via ERGs at various companies!

You never know who will be your next boss or who will connect you to an opportunity that changes your life. That's why being visible with people outside of your team matters, too. Because *that* is how you spread your personal brand like cholera in the 1800s. The more people at your organization who speak highly of you, the more that will be seen as the truth.

LIKABILITY AND VISIBILITY IN THE JOB HUNT

These likability and visibility hacks aren't just good for the workplace—they can help accelerate your job-hunting efforts as well.

Being likable in the interview process really comes down to how easy you are to work with and speak to. Feel free to go back to chapter 6 if you need a refresher on actual interview preparation. Otherwise, follow these likability tips:

- Reply to emails and interview requests quickly.
- Double-check for typos in your emails and application.
- Be clear and direct about what you're looking for and any questions or concerns you have.
- Don't skip the small talk.
- Always say thank you.

As for visibility, stay at the top of the recruiter's mind. This doesn't mean you need to be a LinkedIn influencer, but being active on LinkedIn and engaging with content and people connected to your target company will keep your name popping up on their home screen. It also means you actively send thank-you emails and follow up if you haven't heard back. And for those jobs you don't get, it means you stay in touch.

GAB CLASS

If you've followed me online for a while, you've probably seen my viral series, Gab Class, in which I, a certified yapper, teach you how to talk to anybody without feeling anxious. None of these personal brand hacks will hit if you're not able to hold a meaningful conversation, so it's crucial to develop your ability for small talk.

I hear from executives all the time that it feels like the art of conversation and small talk is dying with the younger generation. My hot take is that the art of conversation is alive and well. The issue is millennials and Gen Zers have seen employers play so dirty over the last ten-plus years that they don't want to play pretend and have fake-ass conversations just to pump the egos of some executives. They're over it. Frankly, so am I.

But that's not what Gab Class is about. Gab Class is about being comfortable chatting with anyone anywhere—in an interview, on the job, or at networking events. (And also on dates, but I'll save that for another book.)

The reason most people get nervous when it comes to speaking to strangers, both professionally and personally, is that they give themselves way too much credit. I mean this in the kindest way possible: You aren't that important. Everyone around you is living a complex life, riddled with their own insecurities and personal struggles. You're only on their mind when you're in front of them. Really sit with how freeing that is. No one gives a shit! You stumbling over your words in a conversation isn't something anyone but you is going to remember. People rarely remember what you say—they remember how you make them *feel.* And *that* is what Gab Class is all about. This is the art of small talk.

You already learned the basics of confident communication and improv theory in chapter 7, so I won't harp on about that. Ground yourself with a calming breath, adjust your body language, act like you've been here before, and let's begin with what a healthy conversational flow looks like:

1. **Be the opener as much as possible.** The trick to feeling less awkward while talking to strangers is to be the person to start the conversation. This gives you an opportunity to mentally prepare and feel in control of the conversation. Whether it's with your empty coffee cup or approaching a senior leader at the company social, the more power you give yourself, the better.

2. **Start with a compliment or question.** This is the easiest way to break the ice. Interestingly, people are more likely to like you when they feel like they've helped you out. (This is sometimes called the Ben Franklin effect, because Franklin wrote about it in his autobiography.) People are also more likely to enjoy you when you compliment them. The easiest (and most professional) openers include:

   - "Hello! I don't think we've met before. I just wanted to say hi." OK, technically, this is neither a compliment nor a question, but it works.

   - "Hello! I just noticed your [book bag, glasses, mug, blazer, etc.]. I just had to tell you that I love it!"

   - "Hi! This networking event has been great. Have you been to others in the city?"

- "Question for you: Do you know where the [activity at the event] is going to be happening?"

3. Inquire and validate. A conversation is really just an exchange of inquiry and validation. Every time the person you're speaking to says something, you reply by either validating them or asking a follow-up question. For example:

   - "That's amazing, good for you! That trip sounds incredible."
   - "Wow, that's a huge accolade! Congratulations!"
   - "Oh, that sounds like a lot of fun. It's great that you and the family did that."
   - "That sounds exhausting. Thank goodness tax season is over."
   - "Interesting, do you think you would do that again?"
   - "What do you mean by [X]?"
   - "What was your favorite part?"
   - "Did [person] also enjoy the experience?"

4. Ask for what you want and get out. Based on how this conversation goes, you can either ask to stay connected with this person via LinkedIn, ask for a more formal career conversation, or simply end it. The secret to being a great conversationalist is not to let things get awkward. That means you need to know when to wrap it up. When the conversation starts to die, say, "It was so good chatting! I'm going to [refresh my drink, say hi to so-and-so, etc.], but I'll see you soon." It's best to give people a short and sweet exchange that leaves them wanting more.

It's important to call out that, especially when talking to someone for the first time at work, you should be focused on being *interested*, not *interesting*. If you want people to like you, you need to shift the focus onto them and encourage them to talk about themselves. The goal is not for you to show off or dominate the conversation. The goal is to genuinely learn about someone and make them feel validated and heard. That's how you develop a great personal brand.

Small talk is a gateway to big connections. So even at the beginning of meetings, don't skip this shit. Here are my favorite small-talk topics:

- Do you have any travel booked?
- Any plans for the weekend?
- Have you been watching [non-scandalous TV show]?
- How are things in your world?
- How is/are your [partner, kids, parents, etc.]?

Ideally, if you talk to the right strangers at work, you may run into them again, in the office or virtually. At that point, you're able to build more rapport, ask follow-up questions, and eventually . . . ask them for favors when needed. Everyone you make small talk with is a potential referral or connection to your next job. Small talk is an essential part of being liked and visible.

Think about how the conversation goes when you see a close friend of yours. There's some great banter, laughs, and questions about relevant things happening in your life. You may ask each other about work, dating, how that dentist appointment went, and so on. You have lore. You have topics to follow up on. At work, it's harder to do this, because you encounter so many people, and unfortunately, you'll find many of them boring. (We're all boring to someone!)

I have a very effective strategy for this, but it's kind of creepy. Is this a safe space? I recommend keeping a (very well-hidden) list of the things people at work tell you. For example, let's say you chatted with Mei Li, the senior finance manager, at your company social. Mei Li mentioned she has one son, Dylan, who is eleven and plays the drums. She also mentioned she hates cooking, so she's been trying out a meal-delivery service. I legitimately want you to write this down in a Word doc or in the Notes app on your phone, because next time you see Mei Li, you're going to ask her how Dylan is doing in his rock-star era and if that meal-delivery service was worth it. You're going to impress the hell out of her because not only did you remember what she told you, you cared enough to follow up. Mei Li may know nothing about the quality of your work, but she knows you make her feel seen, so the next time she has a cool project, you're the person she's thinking of first.

The real secret to being a good conversationalist? Recognize that the conversation is all about *the other person,* especially in your first few conversations. The reason really great conversationalists feel no anxiety speaking to strangers is that they know the secret to being a good conversationalist is not to say the perfect thing but to be quiet and listen—which is actually super easy.

BRINGING IT ALL TOGETHER

Ultimately, your personal brand has much less to do with you than it has to do with how others experience you. Clearly defining who you are and baking that into how you show up and communicate will unlock connections and opportunities that people who are simply flailing through life won't get. Stay likable and visible, master the basics of small talk, and you'll supercharge your personal brand and your career.

CHAPTER 9

BE GREEDY

Welcome to the chapter about the almighty dollar. Consider this a crash course in negotiating job offers, raises, and promotions. With your newfound confidence and sparkling personal brand, it's time to get you paid.

One of my career-coaching clients was a twenty-two-year-old woman in Silicon Valley. Let's call her Natalie. She was an incredibly talented software engineer who was looking for her first role after college, ideally at a tech giant like Apple or Amazon. Like most other new graduates, Natalie worried about which jobs she was qualified to apply to, how to prepare for interviews, and how to network. But without a doubt, her most significant source of anxiety was around knowing which opportunity to accept and how to get paid what she was worth. Prior to our sessions, she often told recruiters that she would accept whatever they offered because it was her first job out of school. To be clear, everyone deserves to be paid fairly at every stage of their career. There is no appropriate time to offer a "discounted rate" because you're new to something.

Another client, Rakesh, was a twenty-six-year-old marketing consultant for a reputable ad agency in Toronto. In our sessions, his primary source of stress was around his salary. He'd been showered with positive feedback from his boss and wanted to stay at his current company, but he hadn't gotten a raise he was expecting. His boss, in my professional opinion, sounded like a bit of an asshole. Rakesh was scared to ask for a raise, even though he knew he was being underpaid, because there was a chance his boss would get testy. You and Rakesh don't need to accept a temperamental boss or an organization that is "tight on budget" as an excuse for being paid below the market rate. Their poor planning shouldn't be impacting your pocketbook.

My advice? Be greedy! No more feeling scared, guilty, or embarrassed to ask for what you deserve. No more having empathy for the excuses companies give you. Effective immediately, your priority is *you*, not some corporation or CEO.

In case you need a kick in the butt, let's talk dollars. Studies show that individuals who skip salary negotiations miss out on up to $1 million in lifetime earnings. ONE MILLION DOLLARS. Additionally, a study conducted by Payscale, a compensation software and data company, showed that 75 percent of people who asked for a raise received a pay increase.

So stop feeling guilty asking for more, stop feeling shame for negotiating your worth. This is business, baby, and leaving *one million dollars* on the table is bad business. This chapter can't start until you give yourself permission to be greedy.

REALITY CHECK: Systemic barriers are very real, so I don't want to imply that getting a raise is as simple as just asking for it. For example, BIPOC women are often labeled "aggressive" during corporate negotiations. My hope is to push everyone to advocate for themselves as much as they're comfortable—and to exhort people not to discriminate when they started making managerial decisions.

THE ART AND SCIENCE OF NEGOTIATION

For such a valuable skill, there sure is a lot of anxiety about being able to negotiate. When many of my clients hear the word *negotiation*, there's an immediate anxiety-induced response that sounds like:

- "What am I, the wolf of Wall Street? I don't want to be aggressive!"
- "I don't want them to think I'm demanding or difficult."
- "I hate conflict. I can't do this!"

To which I respond: Who said anything about being aggressive, demanding, or combative? Negotiation is a dance, not a duel. You've been watching too many HBO shows. Yes, on TV, negotiations always seem to involve two characters with strong personalities in a dramatic emotional conflict, because that's what makes good television. In the real world, emotion is the killer of sound negotiations. So, no, you don't need to be a cutthroat Logan Roy type in order to get what you want; in fact, I'd argue you *shouldn't* be.

A negotiation is just a conversation set to express your boundaries and desires. That's it.

And all great negotiators follow a few fundamental rules:

1. There is no room for emotion in negotiation.
2. Put nothing in writing, ever.
3. Know your worth (and add a bit of tax).
4. Know your walk-away point.
5. Be direct about what you want, then shut up.

Let's go through each rule one by one.

1. THERE IS NO ROOM FOR EMOTION IN NEGOTIATION

There's nothing wrong with having big feelings about a difficult conversation. You may be feeling anxiety, frustration, anger, hopelessness. Your boss might make you want to scream. All of that is normal. Your feelings are completely valid. You're allowed to feel them. But then you need to put them on ice, because walking into a negotiation with too much emotion will cloud your judgment, affect your delivery, and diminish your results.

I don't say this to be harsh. I say this because I care about you. If you're familiar with my content online, you probably know I am a self-identified softie who is highly emotional. So this advice doesn't come from a place of judgment. Rather, this is the advice that has helped both me and my clients get incredible results, even while feeling scared.

Without a doubt, the most common emotion surrounding negotiation is fear—fear of being perceived poorly or rejected. You're worried you're violating social rules and doing something that will be seen as rude or offensive.

As an HR expert, I have news for you: You're not.

Negotiation is a very regular part of business. It is quite literally part of the job of every recruiter, manager, and HR representative to navigate negotiations every single day. They literally get paid to do this. This is their job. You negotiating isn't unique or the exception, it's the norm. In my own experience, something like 97 percent of the candidates I made offers to negotiated. It's that common.

The worst thing they can say is no, and any company worth working at is never going to reprimand you for negotiating your worth. Many people are terrified that if you ask for what you want, you run the risk of the company taking away the offer or promotion because you've been "too greedy." To be clear, this does happen, although very rarely. It may not feel like it at the time, but in the very unlikely event that your offer gets pulled because you negotiated, trust me, it was a dodged bullet. Any company that will punish you for advocating for yourself is not a company you want to be at. If this is how they treat you in the *offer process* (the point where they should be trying to win you over), imagine how they'll treat you over the course of your career.

Negotiation only feels personal for you. The other party is negotiating on behalf of the organization; they aren't paying you directly out of their pocket. Yes, occasionally you might run into some immature or toxic person trying to do *Succession* cosplay, but usually, it won't be personal unless you make it personal by bringing too much emotion into it.

So let yourself feel the feelings, then take a deep breath, and set them aside. Trust me, this isn't as scary as you think.

2. PUT NOTHING IN WRITING, EVER

Have you ever been texting with a friend and sent over a cheeky little joke that immediately started a fight between the two of you? It's a universal experience. If you delivered that joke in person, your friend would be laughing along with you, but things like tone and intention get lost in translation over text.

The same can be said for negotiations. Never, *ever* make your ask in writing. Negotiations are best done in person, on a video call, or over the phone. No exceptions.

3. KNOW YOUR WORTH (AND ADD A BIT OF TAX)

In order to get the results you want, you have to *know* what results you want. Without a clearly defined goal, your negotiation efforts will go to waste. You're just throwing things at a wall and seeing what sticks. How specifically do you determine this number? I'll get to that in just a moment.

4. KNOW YOUR WALK-AWAY POINT

Know what your bare minimum is to accept the opportunity. If you don't get it, be prepared to walk away. Remember, boundaries mean nothing if you aren't willing to enforce them. (Again, more on how to determine what this number should be in a moment.)

5. BE DIRECT ABOUT WHAT YOU WANT, THEN SHUT UP

In order to get what you want, you need to act like you deserve it. Overexplaining and rambling scream, "Please see my worth, I beg of you!" A confident person would never feel the need to convince someone of their value. Instead, they make a clear and direct ask and then sit comfortably in silence. You've already proven that you're worthy of this opportunity simply by having something to negotiate. You don't need to perform anything.

NEGOTIATING A NEW JOB OFFER

You've applied for jobs, networked your butt off, aced some interviews, and now you have a job offer in hand! Proud of you. Let's dive into how to evaluate the job offer and negotiate using our negotiating rules.

The real secret is that negotiation starts before you ever get an offer. With your help, the recruiter has already attached a shiny price tag to your head as early as the first interview. They usually get a sense of your salary expectations by asking you questions like "What are you targeting in your next role?" or "What are your salary expectations?" When a recruiter asks you these things in an interview, I advise you to either put the question back onto them by saying, "I'm flexible for the right role. Are you comfortable sharing your budget?" or say, "Based on where I am in my career, a move would only make sense for me if it's starting at [X amount]." The first option helps you gather the overall salary range for the role, which can determine what is in the realm of possibility. The second is much more direct and transparent, which can help the recruiter advocate for your salary needs and prevent you from wasting time.

If you choose to share your desired salary, never share a range, only the lower limit, because that gives you the freedom to change your mind during the process. I would avoid sharing your current salary with the recruiter. Honestly, it's none of their business, and they may even use that to try and lowball you. If they really push for your current salary, inflate it a bit (by 5 to 10 percent). But never, ever pull a Natalie (sorry, girl, love you). Don't communicate that you're willing to accept anything and have no number in mind—it's only going to bite you in the ass later.

Now, I understand that based on life circumstances, sometimes you simply need to accept the offer in front of you to keep the bills paid. But if you have any choice in the matter, remember that not all offers are worth accepting. Let's go step-by-step through the process of evaluating a job offer and negotiating to improve it—or at least making sure you stay as protected as possible if you need to accept the job either way.

STEP 1: REVIEW THE OFFER AT HAND

Before you can negotiate, you need to understand what the offer in front of you actually looks like. Not all job offers are created equal, and not taking the time to read the fine print of your offer letter can royally screw you over in the future. So step 1 is to actually read every single word of the job offer. A job offer usually includes the following information:

- Start date: This is the date when you start the role.
    - Ask yourself: *Does this timing work for me?*

- End date: If it's a contract position, this is when the role ends.
    - Ask yourself: *Does this length of time align with what I want?*

- Hours: This outlines how many hours you work per week and any overtime allowances.
    - Ask yourself: *Is this what I expected? Will I be required to work a lot of overtime without additional pay?*

- Vacation, sick days, leave, etc.: There should be a detailed overview of what time off you're entitled to.
    - Ask yourself: *How many vacation days will I get? Do I get more the longer I stay at the company? Do they roll over if I don't use them? Do I get paid out if I don't use them? How many sick days do I have? What is the policy on medical leave and parental leave?*

- Probationary period: Most organizations have a thirty-to-ninety-day trial or probationary period during which your employer can terminate you without notice. You might not have full access to company perks and benefits during this time, so pay attention to how this section is written.
    - Ask yourself: *Is this period a fair length of time? Am I willing to absorb this risk?*

- Noncompete clause: This is any clause that prevents you from working at competing companies or even in the same industry after you leave this role. Now, these are generally hard to enforce legally, but if there's a noncompete clause in your offer letter, there's always a risk of legal action should you opt to work for a direct competitor after you leave this job.
    - Ask yourself: *Am I willing to absorb this risk for the opportunity?*

- Compensation: This is your base pay plus any bonuses, stock options, and so on. This is generally the most important element of the offer, so we'll talk about it in full detail in the next section.

- Benefits: These are company-provided benefits like health insurance, dental insurance, a retirement account, and so on.
    - Ask yourself: *Will this leave me uninsured for any length of time? Are the benefits going to cover the most important parts of my lifestyle? Are there any financial benefits, like retirement matching?*

- Reimbursements: If you have to pay for certain expenses out of pocket—for example, while traveling in a role that requires it—there may be a clause outlining what the company covers and how they pay you back.
    - Ask yourself: *Am I going to lose my own money on work expenses?*

- Intellectual property: The offer will usually lay out if the work you do in the role will be owned by you or the company. Depending on your industry, this may be a deal breaker. For example, if you're a visual artist and the company owns any art you create while working for them, that may impact your future usage rights to your own work.

- Ask yourself: *Will these clauses impact my future work or portfolio?*

- Contingencies: This is a list of things your job offer is contingent on. This usually includes employment verification, criminal background check, and sometimes even a credit score check. This one is out of your control, tbh, but don't let it freak you out. They usually don't ask for performance recommendations from your previous employers, just for confirmation that you worked there.

Any time you get an offer letter, review each of these clauses to make sure it's aligned with your expectations and fueled by your VPL (remember, that's your values, purpose, and lifestyle). No matter how shiny and exciting this offer may seem, read through each element to make sure there are no hidden surprises.

There are other factors to consider that may or may not be spelled out in your offer letter. What are the company's policies on working in office versus remotely? How long is your commute and how much will it cost you? Do you have to wear a uniform, and if so, do you have to pay for it yourself? Sometimes because of a job's location, uniform, or travel requirements, you may end up spending more than you save to keep up. Make sure you plot this out before accepting an offer.

STEP 2: CONDUCT EXTERNAL RESEARCH

Successful negotiation is highly reliant on your ability to prepare. Once you receive the offer, thank the recruiter and let them know you'll review it and get back to them "within the next day or so." This buys you time to review while still indicating your interest. (If a company tries to pressure you to say yes right away, that's a massive red flag.)

Now is the time to research the *total compensation*, not just the salary. Of course, the salary is arguably the most important component of the offer, but it can be misleading at times. For example, which offer sounds better to you?

- Offer 1: $180,000 base pay
- Offer 2: $130,000 base pay, 25% year-end bonus contingent on performance, $30,000 in stocks

Offer 1 has guaranteed annual earnings of $180,000, which is great. Offer 2 may initially turn you off because the base pay is significantly lower, but the total value of the offer could be $192,500. The risk with offer 2 is that your year-end bonus is contingent on performance, so it's not guaranteed, plus stocks (although great) aren't liquid, so having $30,000 in stocks is not like having an extra $30,000 in your bank account that you can spend whenever you want. There is no "wrong" offer to accept here; it just comes down to your risk appetite for year-end payouts and how long you plan to stay at a company (because stocks tend to have a vesting period). Personally, I would be taking offer 2. Knowing I have the potential to earn more year over year *and* have stocks building equity for me over the course of the two to four years I tend to stay at companies is valuable to me.

With all that being said, how do you know that your offer is fair based on total compensation?

The first thing you need to do is go to a website like Payscale or Glassdoor to determine what the average salary is for your specific job title and level in your geographic location. These websites will usually offer a fairly accurate range that can help you determine where you fall within the banding. The external market range is really the most important data point in determining your ideal compensation, but you should also factor in personal needs such as your current salary, cost of living, and savings goals.

For example, let's say you've received an offer for a financial analyst position in Toronto with a base pay of $76,000, a year-end bonus of 5 percent, and no stocks. Your online research shows the range for this position is $70,000 to $95,000 with bonuses between 5 and 15 percent, and limited information is available about stocks. (It's important to note that most large companies have less room to negotiate on stocks and year-end bonuses, as those tend to be set and standardized organization-wide, whereas hiring managers tend to have a bit more control over base pay.) The good news is that this offer is in the right range, which is a decent indicator you've got a fair offer on your hands.

Note: Even if an offer is fair, you're still going to negotiate. The worst-case scenario is they say no and your offer stays the same. The best-case scenario is you make more money, and I love that for you.

And I have some good news to report: Many states and provinces are starting to introduce salary transparency laws that require organizations to disclose a salary range in job descriptions. This is a huge win for you, because it can help you understand their budget without having to guess.

STEP 3: DETERMINE YOUR WALK-AWAY POINT AND IDEAL SALARY

Based on your personal financial goals and the market rate you researched in step 2, what is the absolute lowest offer you're willing to accept? In addition to that, what is your ideal salary? Running with the above example, maybe the lowest you're willing to accept is $80,000 and your ideal (realistic) salary is $85,000.

With any new job offer, you should be aiming to increase your earnings as much as possible. Think of each new job as an opportunity to financially upgrade your life. Try to avoid moving into a job with a very small pay increase—or worse, a decrease—from what you're making right now, unless the opportunity is truly worth the cut for some other reason.

STEP 4: CALL THE RECRUITER

Reach out to the recruiter over email to request a time to speak on the phone, because, again, we do *not* negotiate over email. You can say something like: "Thank you again for sending over the offer and for the incredible hiring experience. I wanted to see if you have some time for us to review the offer over a call." They'll respond and schedule a time to speak.

Before this call, take some slow, deep breaths, ground yourself, and repeat after me:

- Handling negotiations is part of the recruiter's job. This isn't anything unique or special.
- The recruiter deals with negotiations every single day and expects it.
- It is not inappropriate for me to advocate for myself.
- I am in this position because I deserve to be.
- This company isn't doing me any favors by giving me a job offer. They are paying me for a service I provide.

When you get on the phone, this is the script you're going to follow:

YOU: Thank you so much for making the time to speak with me! You and the entire team have been so helpful. I'm excited to chat through things, because I'm really interested in the role. I wanted to talk through some questions I had in terms of the offer.

THEM: That's great, I'm happy to!

YOU: Thank you! [Ask less pressing questions, maybe about vacation, probation, or anything else on the offer that stood out. For example: "I noticed vacation is two weeks. Is there any way to bump that up to three?" or "What's the company policy on probationary periods?"]

THEM: (Answer.)

YOU: Thank you! I also wanted to talk a bit about the compensation. I know in the interview process we spoke a bit about salary. Based on where I'm currently at in salary and the external market, I wanted to know if there was an opportunity to increase the base pay?

THEM: Do you have a number in mind? I can check with the manager.

YOU: Based on the research I've done and my current earnings, I would be looking to get as close to $85,000 as possible. [Alternatively: For the move to make sense for me, I'd be considering $80,000 or more but am targeting closer to $85,000.]

THEM: Let me get back to you.

Notice how you didn't re-explain your value because you already know that the company thinks you're great, given they've extended an offer? Notice how you were direct and clear with your asks and then allowed the recruiter to take the lead? I can't overstate enough how important silence is. The most powerful negotiation tool in the world is silence. Make your ask, then be quiet. The ball is in their court.

From there, the recruiter is going to work with the hiring team, potentially check in with the finance team, and get back to you. Based on what they come back with, you may need to do one more round of negotiations to get the number up higher, or they may be clear it's the final offer.

STEP 5:
ACCEPT OR DECLINE

Being anchored in your minimum acceptable offer will make this decision so much easier. Remember, you should be reviewing the total compensation but also the company culture, policies, benefits, and time off. Money isn't everything. It's a lot, but not everything. In addition to the final compensation presented, it's a good idea to ask yourself the following before signing:

- Do I have a clear vision of how performance is managed at this company?
- What does career growth look like here?
- Do I align with the values of the company?
- Will I be expected to work a lot of overtime?
- What is the work-life balance like?
- Did I like the people I met during the interview process?

- Does the company have good reviews on websites like Glassdoor?
- Am I satisfied with the nonmonetary elements of the offer?
- What does time off look like? Are things like parental leave covered?
- Does this company have a track record of doing layoffs or firing people a lot?

If any of the above prompts give you pause, go back to the recruiter to ask questions. Remember, you are the prize here. You're allowed to be picky, even in a bad job market. If you opt to accept the offer, you can email or call the recruiter and make sure to extend your genuine thanks. They love that.

If, for whatever reason, you've decided this isn't the right opportunity for you, you can email or call the recruiter to let them know. Both are uncomfortable. Just like a breakup, doing it over the phone is more respectful, but sometimes schedules don't align. Regardless of the path you go, say something like this:

> I wanted to reach out with a genuine thank-you. You and the team have been incredible throughout the entire process. Unfortunately, I wanted to let you know that I've made the decision not to move forward with this offer right now. [Insert politely phrased reasoning if needed.] I would love to stay in touch for the future, and again, thank you!"

That's really it. If you handle the decline with grace, I promise no one is taking it personally. It's just business.

What If You Have Multiple Offers?

If at any point in the process you have fair offers from more than one company, it's OK to say that you have other offers at play and to share what they're coming in at (and even inflate it a little, if needed). This can push a company to move faster, be more competitive, or even match a higher offer.

When you hop on the phone to negotiate with the recruiter, you can say something like: "I wanted to let you know that I recently received an offer from [X] for [Y] role. I've really been enjoying this interview process, so I wanted to be transparent about my status. Is there anything I can do to support you in terms of timing or sharing salary details?" This is a nice way to say, "If you want me, move quickly and pay me more." As long as you're transparent, clear, and kind in your delivery, you're going to be just fine.

YOU ONLY NEGOTIATE ONCE

There's a saying: "You only negotiate your way in once." It means the most bargaining power you'll ever have at a company is when you're first joining it. It's true, largely because of how organizations distribute salary budgets.

A little-known secret is that the budget for hiring new people and the budget for giving existing employees a raise are usually two very separate things. On average, existing employees see a base pay raise of anywhere from 3 to 5 percent annually, whereas new hires are offered salaries that are competitive with the current external market. This is why I'm a big advocate for leaving your job every couple of years. You maximize your earnings by entering a new organization much easier than you do by growing at your existing one. We'll get into how to negotiate for a raise or a promotion in the next chapter, but without a doubt, the most negotiating power is found in a new job offer, so don't miss your opportunity.

BRINGING IT ALL TOGETHER

Negotiating for your worth is undoubtedly scary and can feel overwhelming, but asking to be paid what you're worth isn't scandalous or "too much." It's just business. You deserve to advocate for your earnings, and if you follow the roadmap in this chapter, you'll be much more comfortable having these conversations. There can be very real challenges around how these conversations are received based on factors like race and gender, but being equipped to navigate them can help.

CHAPTER 10

GROWING YOUR CAREER

At this stage you've got all the skills you need to land a new gig or promotion while being highly visible and likable at work. So once you've secured a new job, how can you continue to grow your career without hating your life?

This chapter is going to cover how to ace your first few weeks in a new role and how to use that momentum to grow your career at this company through promotions and raises.

STARTING A NEW JOB

The first thirty days at a new job sets the tone for your time at the company. This is a unique period of time when you're able to shape your company's impression of you with an entirely clean slate. It's exciting, but also a little intimidating.

"What if people don't like me and I have a hard time making friends?"

"What if there's so much to learn that I fall behind and can't deliver?"

These anxieties are a natural (and very solvable) part of your career.

I had a client named Melanie who recently started a new product manager job at a large tech company and echoed these anxieties. I'll tell you what I told her: The reality is, your boss won't expect you to hit the ground running right away, nor will your peers. On average, it takes three months to be onboarded into a new role and up to six months to start feeling settled. Don't put pressure on yourself to have it all figured out right away. No one does, and no one is expecting that of you.

In my coaching session with Melanie, I shared a very specific timeline that eliminated so much uneasiness because it empowered Melanie to focus on one goal at a time instead of feeling like she was behind on everything with no clue where to begin. I'll share it with you too now.

BEFORE YOU START THE JOB

As you prepare for your first day on the job, do the following:

- Review how you defined your personal brand in chapter 8 and remember to show up as *that.*

- Remember that visibility and likability are king here, so come ready to schmooze.

- If you're in office rather than remote, figure out your route to get there so you're not hit with surprises on day one.

- Creep the company Instagram and other socials to see how employees dress, then lay out an outfit slightly more formal—better to be a tad overdressed on day one.

- Pack a lunch, but expect that you might be taken out for lunch by your boss.

- Most importantly, leave that self-doubt nonsense at the door. You have this opportunity because you deserve it, not because of luck. They're lucky to have you, not the other way around.

THE FIRST THREE WEEKS

The goal of your first three weeks on the job is to learn as much as possible and meet as many people as possible. That is it. You aren't expected to be fully up and running. But by the end of this period, the people around you should see you as likable and competent. Here is your official checklist to complete by the end of week three:

- Finish all of your assigned training and onboarding documentation. It's boring, so get it out of the way.

- Meet as many people as possible, with the support of your boss. Remember, your boss is the ultimate gatekeeper of your career, so you want their buy-in on your actions until they explicitly tell you that you don't need to ask them for permission. This may sound silly and old-school, but you should ask your boss if they're OK with you reaching out to people for coffee chats. I personally have been slapped on the wrist by a previous manager for reaching out to leaders for career chats without their permission, and it started our relationship off on an awful foot. Ideally, meet with significant leaders at the company, the people you'll be collaborating with, and other notable folks around the organization. Treat these as exploratory chats so you can learn more about the work they do and how you'll interact. If you really want to shine, ask them what their ideal partnership with you will look like. Show up with a notebook and a good attitude and be ready to small-talk.

- Be a sponge. The benefit of starting a new job is having fresh eyes on everything and everyone around you. Pay attention to how people work. What processes are broken that you can help fix later? Who are the important people? Do people communicate most on email or messenger? Who is well respected here, and how do they behave? How political is this company, and who will you need on your side? Using this time to absorb the existing culture is going to keep you from fumbling later.

- Ask your boss if you can shadow strong performers on your team to observe how they work (and how they don't).

- Arguably most importantly, pay attention to the people around you and choose which relationships to build. This *never* means you should be rude or dismissive to anyone. Always assume the best in everyone and operate from a place of warmth and kindness. But do observe how people work. Do they have a reputation for good work? Do people find them easy to communicate and work with? Or are they difficult to work with or gossiping regularly? Use this information to determine how much time and caution you will take in building (or not building) a given relationship.

WEEK FOUR AND BEYOND

After week four is when the job really starts, so it's time to plan for your deliverables. By the end of this period, your boss should have faith that you're going to be able to handle the position. This is your game plan:

- Sit down with your boss in a one-on-one meeting to determine a sixty- and ninety-day plan for this role. It's a good idea for you to put this proposal together before the meeting and share it with them for feedback; this shows you're proactive. But if you don't have enough information on what is expected of you, it's entirely OK to ask your boss what they would like to see accomplished over the coming weeks. The goal is to make sure expectations of your role are clear, at least for the next few months.

- Align with your boss on performance management. There is nothing more soul crushing than busting your ass at a job and then getting feedback from your boss that you aren't meeting expectations. The most common reason this happens is because your boss hasn't clearly laid out the performance expectations for the role. In your meeting, ask your boss to chat through how they measure performance to ensure you're being kept on track.

- Ask your boss for feedback. Obviously, you've just started this job, so this is low-key a trick question. When you ask someone for feedback, it makes you look humble and eager, which is a great tone to set with your boss.

- From there, the rest is in your hands. Focus on likability, visibility, and keeping that say:do ratio high.

For the record, it's totally normal to hate the hell out of a new job for the first few months. Remember how humans crave doing things that come easily to us? A new job with all new people and a brand-new routine won't come easily at first, which means it won't exactly boost your confidence. So be easy on yourself. You're not meant to have it all figured out just yet.

WHAT'S NEXT?

Once you stop referring to your new job as "new" and start calling it just your job, it's time to start scheming for what's next. Don't panic—it doesn't mean you need to move jobs immediately. In fact, when possible, staying in your job for at least one year is usually the best call. From a learning perspective, it means you've seen a full cycle in your position, which is great for your development. And from a résumé standpoint, having at least one year in each role builds credibility. So in most cases, taking next steps to move positions when you've been in a role for less than a year usually isn't recommended.

But let's say you've been at your job for a year or so. If you enjoy the company and are keen to stay there, you have two options for your next step. You can move within the company or stay in the same role but ask for a raise. In order to do so, the following must be true:

- You must be well liked at the company.
- You must be visible to your boss.

- You must be good at your job.

- You must know what you want.

Figuring out what's next is harder than we give it credit for. Once you start in your corporate career, it's easy to feel stuck or pigeonholed into one function for the rest of your life. Friendly reminder: That's all capitalist bullshit. You are never stuck, ever. Before you gaslight yourself into thinking you want to stay in your current function or industry, flip back to the Your Dream Life exercise in chapter 2 and reevaluate your VPL. You're allowed to change.

And remember, growth doesn't always need to be upward, so keep an open mind. You can have a full and financially fulfilling career by making lateral moves as well. Sometimes staying at the same job level but moving to a different team or function can round out your experience in a way that will get you paid *handsomely* later. I've seen folks move from sales consultant to marketing consultant and then back to sales but in a management capacity, because they had well-rounded experience after the moves. I've personally moved from HR programs to HR recruitment and found having both channels of experience set me up to be one of the strongest recruiters at the company.

Once you've refreshed your VPL assessment, let's walk you through how to grow at an organization, step-by-step.

STEP 1: DISCOVERY

Without question, the first step in growing at an organization is to have an open conversation with your boss about where you're at. Even if your boss is a useless bag of bones, you need them on your side to help you grow at this company.

When initiating the conversation, say something like this: "I wanted to set some time up to chat through my career development with you. I've so enjoyed my role and learning from you, and I wanted to connect and learn from you in terms of my career planning as I think about the next year or so of my career." This works because you're kissing their ass *and* not saying you want to leave your job tomorrow. If you sound too urgent about this conversation, all they're going to hear is that you're quitting, and they'll be more focused on replacing you than helping you grow. Ideally, share with your boss the specific job you want next or ask for their perspective on what career paths may be a fit. Here are some scripts for you.

- "I wanted to chat because I would love to continue on this team and eventually grow into a team lead role. From your perspective, does that career goal feel aligned? In your opinion, are there areas I should be working on to help me get there? I would love to put together a formal development plan and work together to help me grow in that direction."

- "I wanted to chat because I've been thinking about my next career move, and although I love the work in my role, I was hoping for my next position to be something more social and customer facing. I would love to stay at the company, so I wanted your opinion on what roles may be a good fit."

In both of these examples, you're making your boss a core contributor to your career development, which is what you need. Your boss needs to be genuinely bought into the process so they can help you make connections and manage performance. In the event your boss is a prick and won't help you, that's OK. As long as you keep them in the loop, they won't act as a blocker. (And if they do, the next chapter will help you deal.)

In this conversation, it's also important to ask about your company's promotions and hiring processes, as there may be specific timelines to follow. If your company only reviews promotions in December, that means you need to start making a case for yourself at least five months in advance.

Whether you already know specifically what role you want or you're still figuring that out, the next step is to ask for your boss's recommendation on who to speak to at the company to learn more about their career or function. If your boss is useless, just ask if they're OK with you setting up chats on your own.

STEP 2: LEARN FROM THE EXPERTS

Moving internally to a new role or getting promoted is a bit of a political game, and much of your success relies on how "committed" to the move you appear to be. Taking time to have coffee chats with people internally helps you appear serious about career growth—and it can genuinely be very helpful. Treat these conversations like the ones in chapter 5, with a specific focus on asking:

- What does a day in the life of this role look like?
- What does growth on this team look like?
- What skills or experiences would I need to adopt in order to get on this team or get the promotion?

These conversations will help inform your planning session in step 3.

STEP 3: MAKE A TIME-BOUND PLAN

After having a handful of internal career conversations, you should have a better understanding of the type of role you want. At that stage, book another meeting with your boss with the intention of developing a time-stamped action plan.

You can say something like:

> Thank you so much for all your help! After our conversation, I met with Bob, Suzie, and Olu to learn more about their work. It really solidified my interest in corporate finance as my next career step. I got feedback that in order to get to this position, I should work on my presentation skills and my Excel skills. I wanted to see if you have other feedback based on this. If you're OK with it, can I develop a formal plan that we can use as a guide in our career conversations?

A reasonable boss will usually agree to help. Then it's your job to put together a specific plan. I advise breaking down specific things you'll do or learn by month and then checking in with your boss monthly to provide updates and ask for any additional feedback. The key ingredient to your time-bound plan is to have an end date that your boss is aligned with. Whether you're hoping to get promoted, to have a new job created for you, or to apply for an existing job when it's posted, it's critical to communicate with your boss like so:

> This plan is super helpful, thank you. In your perspective, when do you see me being ready for that next step, and when do we think it'll be a realistic goal to take that next step based on where the company is?

Your boss should respond either by giving a realistic timeline (which would be in the next six to sixteen months) *or* by saying that they don't know. Sometimes you have to wait for a position to be opened or a budget to be approved, and that's out of your boss's control. After that point, make a pact with yourself that you'll wait for X number of months before you start looking for a new job.

STEP 4:
LIVE BY THE 10 PERCENT RULE

The 10 percent rule has fundamentally changed the course of my career and earnings. I know for a fact it will do the same for you, whether you're targeting a new role, a promotion, or a raise. It will help you catapult your career to the next level and, in some ways, recession-proof your job. Knowing what you want out of the next step of your career, there may be experience gaps based on what you're exposed to in your current role. The 10 percent rule can fix that.

This rule challenges you to spend up to 10 percent of your workweek focused on something outside the scope of your job description. Online shopping doesn't count—it needs to be something that will help you get to your ideal next job. For example, when I was working as a senior sales and tech recruiter, my 10 percent was spent supporting the recruitment marketing and social media team because I wanted to eventually move onto their team.

This also meant that if I were laid off, the company I worked at wouldn't just lose a strong recruiter, they would lose a recruitment marketing powerhouse. I dipped my toes in so many projects that if I left, it would be really hard to replace me. I'd argue most of us aren't paid our worth—we're paid based on how hard we are to replace. Working on these extra projects helped me get cozy with the director of marketing, work with the marketing managers, and build a brand reputation for myself on their team.

Now, you shouldn't just go rogue and decide to shadow a team for fun. That's called stalking, and it's not cute. What you're going to do is ask your boss to connect you to opportunities to work on projects that will help you close the skills gaps you agreed on in your previous conversations. This only works if you're absolutely crushing it in your current job and have the capacity to take on more. I understand that if your workload is unmanageable or your boss is a dick, this may be off the table. But I'd then ask: Why do you want to stay at a company that isn't invested in you?

STEP 5:
ASK FOR WHAT YOU WANT

You are the driver of your career. It's no one else's responsibility to check on you and help you get to that next level. Your boss is too busy with their own career growth to take responsibility for yours. If you want something, make a plan to get it, and when it's time, collect what's yours.

This may be as simple as applying for jobs on your internal career site when they pop up and asking your boss to put in a good word. This may mean your boss needs to submit you for a promotion. This may mean you're waiting for a totally new job to be created. Whatever the end goal you've landed on is, having a time-bound plan makes it easy to hold others accountable, because when the end of your planned timeline is approaching, your boss can't act surprised you want a new job. They cosigned this. That means it's your duty to follow up and drive things forward to get the results you want.

BIRTH OF A SALESMAN

I have seen this happen countless times with my clients: They do all the right things—make a plan, network, develop their skills—and still they're passed up for opportunities or told to "wait it out" by a boss who clearly doesn't have their best interests at heart. Although this might be because of a toxic work culture (which we'll address in the next chapter), sometimes it's because you need to become a better salesperson.

One of the most impactful periods of my recruitment career was leading the talent function for a sales team of more than two hundred people. I spent countless hours with the strongest salespeople in the organization, learning what made them so special so I could hire people who possessed those same superpowers. I could write a second book about everything I learned about life during my time as a sales recruiter, because it genuinely rewired my brain.

Adopting a sales mindset in your career is life-changing. It doesn't mean that you're pushy or that you never take no for an answer, because that isn't what the great salespeople do. They don't steamroll or get in your face and force you to buy what they're selling. What they are is consistent. Great salespeople aren't scared to get creative and be persistent to get the job done. I challenge you to start thinking about your career through the lens of a salesperson.

The salespeople who meet and exceed targets are the right kind of crazy. Even during difficult quarters, when they may be behind on targets, they never, ever act defeated. Instead, they become energized by the challenge. They don't blame the tanking economy or unrealistic targets as the reason they're falling behind. Instead, they lock in, activate a sense of competitiveness, and carry themselves like they're going to hit target no matter what. And shockingly, most times, they do. Great salespeople see adversity as a challenge they can overcome, and act accordingly. What this means for you: Be a little crazier. Take ownership of your career growth, and when things feel off track, either redirect the action plan or get out of that job.

Exceptional salespeople always FSO (figure shit out). Seriously. They have the unique ability to say yes to doing new things even when they don't know how they'll accomplish them yet. So much of sales is figuring things out on the fly, which is why new opportunities don't scare them. The more you adopt the mindset of figuring shit out on the fly, the more career-changing opportunities will fall on your lap. Take new opportunities and run with them.

Many salespeople live by the rule of seven, a sales and marketing term that states a customer needs to interact with a brand seven times before they make a purchasing decision. This may mean a person sees two commercials on TV, sees an ad on the subway, sees a sponsored post on social media, gets a call from the sales team, hears a radio ad, and receives an email from the same sales representative before they finally decide to purchase a product. Good salespeople know that asking you to purchase a product once isn't enough. They need to influence you again and again.

Think of your career as your product and your consumer as your boss. Your boss needs consistent and clear messaging that politely reminds them what you want. It's as simple as that. You asking for growth once isn't enough. You need to be having regular career conversations and socializing your ideal next career move at minimum once a month. Look for opportunities to socialize your career desires regularly, and don't get discouraged if it takes a little time.

In a nutshell, to get the career mobility you desire, you need to be highly intentional. You need to be the absolute driver of your career and steer your boss in the right direction. And yeah, you need to be a little crazy. Crazy is good.

ASKING FOR A RAISE

Now you know how to move laterally or upward at a company, but what if you're happy in your job and simply want a raise? Sometimes growth can just be in our wallets.

If you're not getting a raise every single year, you're actually getting a pay cut. If your salary isn't being bumped up to match inflation and the rising cost of living, you're literally being underpaid. Some companies have annual performance reviews where your boss will give you a performance rating that is tied to a year-end bonus or salary increase. Other companies don't have a formal structure for this. So whether you're preparing for year-end performance review season or just tired of being underpaid, this is how you're going to ask for a raise.

First, you already know the drill: Drop the anxiety. You aren't acting inappropriate by asking for a raise, and you shouldn't "just be happy to have a job." You can be grateful for your career and want more from it at the same time. That said, you probably shouldn't ask for a raise if you're not really good at your job.

> **REALITY CHECK:** You have much less bargaining power when asking for a raise at a company you already work at than when asking for a higher salary when you first receive a job offer. Unless you have another job offer in hand or are willing to quit if you don't get your desired raise, you can't be too aggressive with this one.

Similar to the steps for negotiating for a job offer, you're going to start off by doing market research. Go online and see what the average salary for your job is in your city and make note of where you fall within that range. You should also be considering what your personal finance goals are when you determine your ideal raise.

When it feels like you've been in the role long enough and have had enough positive feedback, book a one-on-one meeting with your boss or bake this into a preexisting meeting with them. You're going to say something like this:

> Thanks so much for making the time to speak! I wanted to check in because I'm continuing to love my work here and the team so much. I'm overall really happy. My goal is to keep learning and growing on the team. As the position has continued to grow [or insert another reasoning that isn't just "I want more money"], I wanted to see if there's an opportunity to discuss my salary and the potential of reviewing it based on performance and the changing market.

Then you stop talking. You've already proven your worth every single day by how you show up to this job. Now is not the time to put together a full sales pitch and come in hot. No. You're simply asking a question: "I want a raise. What do you think about that?"

Pay very close attention to how your boss responds. You're likely to get one of the following responses:

- "Thanks for asking. Do you have a number in mind?"
  - *Translation:* "Tell me the number, and I'll let you know if it's reasonable."
  - *Response:* Share your ideal salary. Don't play games. Be direct.
- "Thanks for asking. Let me see what we have in budget, and I'll get back to you."
  - *Translation:* "I'm optimistic this can be done. I'll look into it and let you know what we can squeeze."
  - *Response:* Follow up in a week if you don't hear back.
- "We usually review this during the performance cycle, so I'll make sure to bake that into your review."
  - *Translation:* "This is on the table but not right now. I need to follow the company process."
  - *Response:* Thank them for being open and trust they won't screw you.
- "Maybe that's something we can talk about in the future."
  - *Translation*: "A raise is probably not happening."
  - *Response:* Thank them for keeping the door open and ask if there are any constraints around either

your performance or budget. But realistically, this type of response means you aren't getting a raise.

- "We don't have the budget."
    - *Translation:* "A raise is definitely not happening."
    - *Response:* Thank them for being honest. If you're truly unhappy with your current compensation, this is your sign to start job hunting.

When it comes to asking for a raise, the best approach is to be direct and express gratitude for your boss's time. You don't want to play games or get into an aggressive negotiation. Think about this as having an open conversation with your boss and asking them for help. They'll either help you or they won't. And if you're catching the drift that a raise is never coming or company spending always seems to be "on pause," you need to put yourself first. This may be the push you need to find a new and better opportunity elsewhere.

BRINGING IT ALL TOGETHER

The bottom line? Start treating your career development like it's a regular part of your job. Whether you're starting a new role or working on getting to your next position, operate like it's a strategic function of your role. That means actively tracking your career feedback, leveraging the 10 percent rule, and above all, asking for what you want. If you're waiting on your manager to guide your career journey, don't hold your breath.

CHAPTER 11

PRESERVING YOUR SANITY

There's no other way to start this chapter than with a formal "fuck you" to hustle culture. Fuck the idea that burnout is a badge of honor. Fuck the sense of superiority that people get from working overtime. And fuck the companies that feel entitled to every waking hour of your day.

That was cathartic.

When I say be a little crazy, I mean be daring. I mean act confident even if you don't feel confident. I *don't* mean drive yourself insane by working 24/7 and paying no attention to the other areas of your life. This chapter is dedicated to helping you get ahead in your career without losing your mind.

HUSTLE CULTURE

Your desire to work hard and be successful is a good thing—in moderation! But hustle culture is a very anti-moderation mindset.

The term *hustle culture* actually goes back decades. According to NPR's *Code Switch*, "In the 1990s and early 2000s, Black rappers started to fold the idea of hustling into their lyrics . . . weaving it into a narrative about Black resilience and self-empowerment."

The idea was not to glamorize "the work itself" but rather "the strength and ingenuity needed to toil through this hard work." However, once the corporate world got ahold of it, the meaning began to shift.

With the boom of technology companies in Silicon Valley hunting for funding and the rise of startup culture in the early 2000s, working long hours to win investor buy-in became synonymous with success. That high-intensity, "always on" work culture was contagious and spread to other industries globally. Offices began to offer free food, entertainment rooms, and gyms, not because they wanted employees to take breaks throughout the day but because they didn't want them to leave.

On social media in the 2010s, we saw the mainstreaming of terms like #HustleCulture, #RiseAndGrind, and #GirlBoss, encouraging people to flaunt their hard work and career accolades online. Suddenly, working hard and long hours meant not only visibility at your job but also recognition from your peers online. Combine that with the fact that the 2008 recession and rising economic precarity made "side hustles" necessary for many people just to pay the bills, and hustle culture became a fundamental part of millennial life.

But as Gen Z joins the workforce, they've started to reject the notion of hustle culture. Not because they're lazy, but because they've seen some shit. When they were young, they may have seen their hardworking, meritocracy-loving parents get laid off without notice or severance during the 2008 recession. When they were older, the Covid pandemic affected their education or early careers. To put it simply, Gen Z is more anti-capitalist and less likely to buy into the corporate bullshit (love y'all for that).

Does that mean we can expect to finally lay hustle culture to rest?

Not yet. Because right now, who are the people *managing* Gen Z? And who is managing Gen Z's managers? Millennials, Gen Xers, and Boomers. So although Gen Z depersonalizes work more than other generations, the working world hasn't caught up yet. Gen Z gives me hope that we will see a shift in how we think about work and hustle culture as they continue to move up the ranks, but for now, we're still in the trenches.

All to say, using #HustleHard on an Instagram post might be incredibly embarrassing today, but hustle culture lives on in the way corporations expect you to show up.

BURNOUT

The prominence of hustle culture in the corporate world is directly to blame for the stark increase in cases of burnout. *Burnout* as a term has been thrown around so much that, for me, it almost started to lose its meaning—until I got hit with a serious case of it.

In early 2024, I was juggling my career-coaching business, social media, and a recent promotion to principal recruiter. On paper, my career was thriving. I had it all. Well, except for a will to live.

It started slowly. First, I was just a bit run-down and was convinced I needed to catch up on sleep. But it didn't matter how many hours of shut-eye I got, I woke up dragging my feet. Then I started to create distance from my loved ones; surely, I just needed some alone time to reset. I started skipping the gym to catch up on work and working regularly on weekends to "make the rest of the week lighter." I was skipping the parts of the workday I previously loved, like chatting with my work friends. Above all, I was miserable. I woke up feeling nothing but dread, and I cried after work almost every single day.

I remember calling my dad (while I was an absolute wreck) and asking him what to do. He told me I was burnt out and I needed to treat it like a physical illness before it became one.

The best way to treat burnout is to prevent it. The second-best way is to take time away from work to recover, if you can. And if you're reading this thinking burnout will never catch up to you, I'm here to tell you that you're wrong. No one is immune from the mental and physical ramifications of burnout, because every company, even the "good guys," will work you to the bone (even if it isn't intentional).

As a result of the burnout epidemic, organizations and global health experts started to raise flags. The World Health Organization declared burnout an occupational phenomenon with symptoms including exhaustion, mental distance from work, and diminished productivity.

THE WORK-LIFE BALANCE REBRAND

In a post–Great Resignation world, working sixty hours a week is less of a flex and more of a flop. Working people woke up, largely in response to the pandemic, and realized hustle culture isn't cute. Organizations quickly moved from glamorizing the grind to boasting about the work-life balance they offered.

Work-life balance as a term first gained popularity in the 1970s and '80s when women started joining the workforce at a higher rate and struggled to balance a full-time job with raising a family. This term was used to advocate for more flexible working policies to help all employees balance their work and home lives.

But the problem is, the line between work and life is much thinner today than it was in the '80s. For most corporate roles, you'll have work emails and messages on your phone. You have a laptop sitting on your kitchen counter that you quickly check before bed to "make sure everything is OK for tomorrow." Even if you're only working forty hours a week, you're mentally working every time you look at your phone, without even realizing it.

And yet, corporations still define work-life balance with the same policies they did when disco was alive and well. To them, having fixed hours means you get to go home and be with your family, and free lunches in the office means you're taking appropriate breaks. And sure, benefits and allowances around leaves of absence have generally improved. But the core issue stands. This shit doesn't ever really feel balanced.

Why? Because work-life balance is kind of bullshit.

Over the course of your career, you'll hear people talk about work-life balance like it's a gift a company can give you. Although it's true that some organizations are better than others with respect to your personal life, the only way to have true work-life balance is to take the matter into your own hands. It isn't a balance at all. It's a boundary you get to set and enforce.

Everyone will tell you that with appropriate work-life balance, you can "have it all" and live a stress-free life. And I do think that's true, to an extent. I think you can have it all, *overall.* But you can't have it all, *all the time.*

So, no, you aren't crazy for feeling like you're "work-life-balancing wrong." You've just been chasing a pipe dream. Of course you constantly feel like you're slacking with friends or family or work or education. You always feel like something's being sacrificed because it is. The scales will almost never feel evenly balanced, and that's normal. What gets more attention is based on what matters most at that point in your life. Work-life balance is an aggregate goal.

The challenge is finding a healthy balance between your personal life and professional life while still getting ahead in your career.

The old-school train of thought tells you that to be successful you need to work long hours, be the first to arrive in the office and the last to leave, reply to email on the weekends, and be a nonstop working machine. I won't lie to you. If you do those things, it's possible you will get ahead faster; you're doing more and being seen more than most. But that way of living isn't sustainable. Doing it all, all the time, isn't a long-term solution. Studies show that productivity and quality of work drop significantly when we work more than fifty hours per week. You will burn out, be miserable, and get sick.

As a rule of thumb, when you start a new job, you should, to some extent, prioritize work. Perception is everything, and being seen as someone who takes extra-long lunches, rolls up to the office late, and heads out at three isn't the first impression you want to make. Essentially, until you have a strong brand reputation, operate with a bit more rigor and at least pretend that work is your priority. This doesn't mean working yourself to the bone, it just means working smarter.

- Show up at nine and leave at five. If you're more junior on the team, ask if anyone needs help with anything before you head out. (I once worked with a coordinator who supported a recruiter, and that coordinator left every day at 3 p.m. even though the recruiter was in the office until 6. She didn't last long.)
- Take your legally entitled breaks, but don't give yourself an extra-long lunch early on.
- Schedule an email or two to be sent at 5:15 so there's a perception you're working hard but not willing to do egregious overtime.
- If something important needs to be done that may require you working up to thirty minutes late, do it.
- Even when things are quiet at work, don't tell people that you have nothing to do.
- Look busy when you're in public, even if that means typing fake emails during slow periods.

As you grow and get more comfortable at a company, you can have more autonomy over your day. But start off slightly conservative—emphasis on the *slightly*, because you also don't want to create the impression that you'll be doing a level of work that would burn you out to maintain.

WORK-LIFE BOUNDARIES

So if work and life aren't ever fully balanced, how do you preserve your sanity? Remember, there will always be a degree of sacrifice in one area or another, even if it's small. It doesn't make the notion of balance any less important. It simply means we need to redefine it. Work-life balance is an active practice of setting boundaries and conditioning people to respect them. It is *not* a corporate program or lifestyle that you adopt—it's an active decision you make every single day so you can live the life you want.

This is why aligning your career choices with your VPL is so important, because expectations vary in each industry. For example, if having time for loved ones and working no more than forty hours a week is important to you, you probably shouldn't be an investment banker. So the first boundary is determining if the industry you want to work in aligns with your lifestyle goals.

And before you start feeling anxiety about being "too junior" or "too new" or "not talented enough" to set boundaries, repeat after me:

- I deserve to be shown respect through how I am treated at work, regardless of where I am in my career.
- I may need to prioritize work for a period of time to get ahead, but that doesn't mean I will let work take over my life.
- Wanting to have a full and meaningful life outside of work doesn't make me lazy.
- Anyone who will shame me for trying to have a life outside of work probably doesn't have a very interesting life themselves.

To be clear, not only do you deserve to have boundaries, you *need* them to get ahead and stay ahead. When you preserve your energy and time, you free up space to focus on the work that really matters.

The most common thief of work-life balance is the number of hours you work, both on the clock and off. Anyone who tells you that you should never, *ever* work overtime is lying to you, because there will definitely be a period of your career where you need to roll up your sleeves and do a little more than what you bargained for. And that's OK, as long as there's an end in sight. Maybe it's a busy month or there's a big project you need to deliver. Working overtime when there's a clear goal and end date is a very normal part of the work experience *if* it is temporary.

If you expect to log off right at five every day for the rest of your career, you're in for some disappointment—but you *should* expect that to be the case about 90 percent of the time. As scary as it feels, you're the only person who can set that boundary. Here's how to protect your time so that 90 percent of your workweeks are healthy:

- **Communicate a busy social schedule.** Let people know that you have places to be and things to do. This could be a real obligation like picking up kids, or it could just be that you have trivia on Tuesdays. Drop it into conversations casually so that people don't expect you'll always be available to stick around. You can fib—maybe you really only have trivia every *other* Tuesday—but don't straight-up lie. And only share activities you truly do so you don't get caught.

- **Block your calendar.** Block the last thirty minutes of your workday in your calendar every single day, so no one can throw in a last-minute meeting or try to trap you with an emergency project. This also buys you time to wrap up any urgent work before the end of the day.

- Turn off work notifications on your phone or have two phones. After you log off, stay logged off. They aren't paying you extra to think about work on your way home. Either turn off email notifications or get a second phone. Every time you check your emails on personal time, you're taking a step back into the office and delaying your ability to unwind. If you don't respect your own boundaries, how is anyone else going to?

- Only reply during working hours. Make a habit to only respond to emails during working hours. You teach people how to treat you. If you start every job replying to emails late at night or on the weekends, you're letting people know that you're OK with that. So either don't reply, set an out-of-office notification that starts at 5 p.m. every day, or respond just to acknowledge the email and confirm you'll get back to them tomorrow.

- Manage your capacity. If the volume of work you're expected to do isn't realistic with the amount of time you have to complete it, you need to take action. Share your concern with your boss and ask if there's "any way we can streamline the process to make it less time-consuming" or anything you should "reprioritize to ensure everything gets delivered on time." A reasonable boss will help you find solutions.

- Say no. Saying no is maybe the most powerful career tool in the world. It's OK to say no to some company socials and after-hours events to conserve your energy. If you're being pulled in hundreds of different directions at work and projects are being thrown at you left and right, it's OK to pause and say, "Thank you so much for sending this over. I may need to work with my boss to balance my capacity. Can I get back to you on this?" If you keep saying yes because you're scared of being seen as difficult, you'll burn out and make more mistakes than necessary—which won't help your reputation in the long run.

TAKE TIME OFF

It goes without saying, but taking time off is so important. When I ask clients experiencing burnout and general job dissatisfaction if they're using their paid time off and sick days, they usually answer no. Calendar-blocking your day to have dedicated IAPNAE time (that's "I'm a person, not an employee" time, in case you've forgotten my extremely pronounceable acronym) is critical. But also, so is logging the fuck off for a week.

Here are the excuses I hear all the time from my clients and how I respond to them:

- "Work is so busy right now, it's not a good time to take a vacation." It's never going to be a good time, so choose a time anyway.

- "I feel guilty taking time off." This company wouldn't feel guilty laying you off if they needed to.

- "I don't want to go on vacation because I know I'll have so much work waiting for me when I return." The work is always going to be there, and with global warming, the beaches literally may not. It's easier to learn how to put work out of your mind for a week or two than it is to deal with burnout.

Stop feeling emotionally tied to your job and start feeling emotionally tied to your life. And if that didn't snap you back into reality, maybe this will: Your paid time off, sick days, and other benefits are literally part of your compensation package, so if you don't use them, you're willingly being underpaid. That's just bad business.

DEALING WITH A TOXIC WORKPLACE

In addition to lack of work-life balance, one of the other biggest factors that leads to burnout is working with people who are manipulative, toxic, or outright mean. You can do all the right things and set all the right boundaries, but if you have coworkers or bosses who are determined to cross them, you're on a one-way train to burnout city. Friendly reminder: Work should not be causing you serious anxiety, dread, and depression.

Working with difficult people is an unavoidable part of life, but difficult and toxic are two different things. A list of things that are not normal from your boss or coworker:

- They take credit for your work and never shout you out for your accomplishments, but when you make mistakes, you're entirely to blame.
- They lash out at you when they're having a bad or stressful day.
- They gossip with you about your peers. (If they talk shit about others when they're not there, they talk shit about you when you're not there.)
- They throw you under the bus for doing what was asked of you.
- Unrelenting micromanagement.

- Unrealistic expectations.
- They constantly give you negative feedback (delivered in a rude way) and are *never* receptive to feedback on their own behavior.
- They block your growth at the company.
- They consistently cross your boundaries.

The list can go on and on, but as a rule of thumb, if someone you're working with makes you feel like an idiot *and* like they never have your back, there's a high likelihood you're in a toxic environment. The second a job starts impacting your mental or physical health, you need to take action. Don't wait for it to get better, because it'll only ever get worse. If you find yourself in a toxic work environment, you have three action items: create distance, communicate, or cut ties.

STEP 1: CREATE DISTANCE

The second you sniff some toxicity at work, whether that be from your boss or your coworkers, your first move is going to be to create distance both in action and in mind.

First, realize that these people are straight-up losers. How people treat you is a reflection of how they treat themselves, so if a coworker or boss is going out of their way to tear you down, they're acting that way because you intimidate them and they're miserable. I know that's blunt, but having worked in human resources, I've seen these people hundreds of times in my career, and the root cause is always the same: It's not you, it's them. So don't you dare internalize their bad behavior and wonder, "What's wrong with me?" The only thing wrong with you is that you're letting these losers get in your head.

Next, get serious about protecting yourself in the office, because if they're the type to sabotage you or try to minimize your accomplishments, you can't let them get in the way of your career growth. You need to CYA (cover your ass).

Remember that no one at work is your friend, not even your work bestie. I know that is tough to hear, but unless you hang out regularly outside of work and *don't* talk about work at all when you're together, that's not your friend. That's your friend from work. And that friend from work will throw you under the bus to save their own ass. So don't start talking shit with your office friends about this toxic person, because I promise it will come back to haunt you. This is a hard pill to swallow, but again, I am HR. I've seen this too many times before.

Limit socializing. If things feel like high school in your company, book workout classes over lunch, or anything else that will prevent you from having to spend social time with these energy suckers.

Document everything. When that toxic coworker or boss asks you to complete a task, document their ask and have them confirm it in writing. These types of people will try to trap you by asking for something verbally and then change the requirements and blame you for "dropping the ball." Instead, when they ask for things verbally say, "Happy to help! I'm just tracking my deliverables, so I'll send you an email summarizing this, and you can let me know if anything is missing." Translation: I'm onto you, you bully.

And when the toxic person makes snide comments toward you, don't react and give them the satisfaction of seeing you crack (or the ammo for them to say you "attacked" them). Instead, play a little stupid. Try saying in a genuine and earnest way, "Sorry, I didn't hear that. Would you mind repeating that?" or "I don't understand what you mean by that." Now they have to double down on their nasty comments. As always, take this advice in context, and don't play dumb if you don't feel safe or if you think you could be punished for it. And in no case should you *ever* react, retaliate, or push back. The goal isn't for you to be passive-aggressive, it's to force the toxic party to say inappropriate things in a very clear way, so you can document what they said and when they said it, for step 2. Having documentation means you can provide specific examples of the issues you've been dealing with, and if HR gets involved, I promise they will ask for it.

STEP 2: COMMUNICATION

Sometimes creating distance and documenting things is enough to keep the crazy at bay. Unfortunately, sometimes it's not. If things are not getting better, the next course of action is to communicate your concerns.

If the toxic person is a coworker, I advise sitting with your boss to share your concerns in an open and empathetic way. You don't want to come across as being difficult to work with, so phrase your concern like this in your next one-on-one meeting: "I wanted to connect to get some feedback. In working with Bobby, I noticed there were a few instances where the requirements for my work changed without notice and some intense supervision of my work was taking place. I wanted to get a sense of if there's anything I'm missing or any advice on how I can better partner with Bobby moving forward."

Your boss will be able to read between the lines here, trust me. You're coming from a place of expressing a genuine desire to collaborate well with Bobby, and you're focused on *you*. When you frame complaints in a way that makes it sound like you're asking for feedback on yourself, you're going to be met with much more empathy. You're basically saying, "Working with Bobby is hell—is it me?" Instead of your boss jumping in to defend Bobby, they're automatically being primed to be on your side because of your humility. It's evil genius. Your boss might offer to chat either with Bobby or their manager, which should be enough of a solution to keep things moving along.

Now, if your boss is the toxic one, that's a different can of worms.

You've heard me preach about the importance of the relationship you have with your boss. They are the ultimate copilot of your career. So if your boss is a toxic nightmare, your career growth and overall wellness are very much at risk. I fear your options are rather limited:

1. You can try to offer feedback to your boss similar to the phrasing above: "I wanted to connect to get some feedback. I so value our partnership and have noticed that in the last project we worked on, there were some bumps in terms of expectations. I wanted to see if there is feedback for me on how I can better deliver." An emotionally intelligent person would then ask you for feedback or offer combined solutions. A total useless doorknob will not. I hope that helps.

2. You can try to go to your boss's boss or to HR. This is a final point of escalation, and depending on your corporate culture, this may or may not go over smoothly. This is only appropriate after several attempts to communicate with your boss and if you're ready to quit. This is where your documentation comes in, as your boss or HR will likely ask for "proof" of your experience. But don't preemptively send an email with a list of all the ways you have been wronged. Instead, hang on to your documentation until they ask to see it.

But if I can speak freely—which I totally can, because it's my book—managing a toxic boss is almost always more trouble than it's worth, even if you bring things up in a very gentle way. Toxic people don't have the ability to self-reflect and act with humility.

STEP 3: CUT TIES

If the situation at your current job is simply too toxic for you to manage on your own, you might just have to find a new job. I am a big believer in something I call ABI (always be interviewing) for this very reason. When you're constantly interviewing for other jobs, it can help you jump ship in case things at work take a turn. In my mind, an emotionally intelligent boss will *want* your feedback and will *want* to constantly be improving your relationship. Unfortunately, people who don't want to change . . . won't. So if your boss isn't receptive to feedback or changing their style of management, it's out of your hands. Sure, you might be able to make it work. But life is too short to shrink yourself for the comfort of jerks. If your boundaries are constantly being crossed and you're in an environment that makes you miserable, you can and should quit your job.

QUITTING YOUR JOB

If a job no longer serves you, either because it's toxic or because it's simply no longer the right fit, it might be time to move on. But before you pull the plug and quit your gig, consider this:

- Have you given this job enough time to settle in? It's normal to hate a job in the first six months.
- Have you done everything you can to have a healthy working relationship with your coworkers and boss?
- If you plan to quit without another job lined up, do you have enough savings to cushion you financially?
- What have you learned you *don't want* so you don't repeat the same cycle in the next job?

If you're genuinely feeling ready to pull the plug, because you're either bored or miserable, hell yeah. If someone warns you of the "risks of job hopping," hop away from them. *Job hopping* is a term used to describe regularly moving jobs, and in a traditional careers book, it would be deemed "unprofessional." This is a capitalist fear-mongering tactic developed because replacing people is expensive and it's cheaper to keep you working for the same company for years than it is to hire someone new. The reality is, moving jobs every two to three years will maximize your earnings. Why the hell would you stay loyal to a company for your entire career if they're not loyal enough to you to provide you a financial incentive to do so?

However, remember how I said many key decision-makers and hiring managers are Gen Xers and Boomers? That means many of them still subscribe to the notion that job hopping is bad. That's why, ideally, you should try to tough out each job for at least a year, ideally two. The odd move sooner than that won't kill you, but to avoid critique from hiring managers, don't make it a habit.

LEAVING FOR ANOTHER JOB

If you've secured a job offer you plan to accept, here's how you're going to tell your current employer.

First, take a second to celebrate! Next, hop on the phone with the recruiter for your new job and ask what contingencies are outstanding on your offer. For example, you might need a criminal background check or credit check to clear before you start the job. Don't submit your resignation to your employer until you feel confident you will pass any checks *and* you've officially signed the offer letter. Nothing is real until it's in writing.

However, if your primary reason for leaving your job is financial, try this. Go to your boss *before* you sign the job offer for the other company and have a fifteen-minute chat, either in person or on the phone. Say this:

> Thank you very much for speaking with me. I wanted to connect because I've been extended an offer for a job I'm really excited about that is a great fit financially. I'm struggling with the decision, which is why I wanted to connect. I love my job and the team here, and I'd love to stay, but financially, this is a great move for me. Do we have any wiggle room for a counteroffer?

This gives your boss a chance to save you by throwing money your way. Nothing wrong with a little bidding war.

Now, if you know *for sure* you want out of this job, sign your new offer and book a fifteen-minute chat with your manager as soon as possible, ideally in the morning. Here's what you're going to say:

> Thanks so much for meeting with me! I wanted to book this time to share some news. I recently received an offer from [X company] for a role and package that is a great step for me. I wanted to let you know I've made the decision to accept the offer. I'm so thankful to you and the team, and this was a hard decision.

Your boss will then respond either like a normal person and congratulate you or like a teenage boy whose Xbox has been taken away. Either way, that's not your problem.

DON'T BURN BRIDGES

How you handle your exit will be the last impression the entire company has of you. I've seen incredible employees destroy years of brand building with how they behaved in the last few weeks of their employment. The world is smaller than you think it is, and you never know who your future boss or recruiter might be, so kill 'em with kindness and competency.

First, determine your last day, in partnership with your boss.

Based on where you live and your employment contract, you may be required to give two weeks or more of notice. The best way to go out is by respecting that period.

Next, work with your boss on a transition plan. This might mean organizing your projects and passing them off to others.

My biggest piece of advice is: Don't act *too* happy. Don't walk around the office jumping for joy and celebrating the fact that you're free from the shackles of this hellhole. Don't totally slack off and do nothing all day, even though you technically have nothing to lose. Act like you still care, even if you don't. Because that's what people will remember: *Even in their last days they were so helpful and kind. It says a lot about them.* Add your peers on LinkedIn to stay in touch and then get the fuck out of there.

BRINGING IT ALL TOGETHER

If you catch yourself in a phase of life where you feel utterly behind in work or your personal life, know you aren't alone. The traditional view of work-life balance is nearly impossible to achieve in our modern, technology-driven world. There will be days when you prioritize career, days when you prioritize family, and days when you prioritize binge-watching reality TV. All of that is OK.

It's not meant to be a perfect balance—it's meant to be whatever helps you feel fulfilled and stay paid. It's meant to be a job that keeps the lights on and fuels the life you want to live. And sure, sometimes that means putting in some extra hours. But it shouldn't mean tolerating disrespect, shrinking yourself, or being terrorized by high school bullies who grew up and moved into corporate. Your boundaries are there to protect your peace; they won't bother anyone except the people who intend to cross them.

So set your standards. Flex your job to fit around your life and not the other way around. And the second you realize your VPL isn't being satisfied, leave. You don't owe these people a thing.

CONCLUSION

A HUG AND A PEP TALK

This book is the amalgamation of everything I wish someone would have told me earlier in my career. It is every single practical tip and mindset shift that I learned after years of being an industry-leading recruiter. It is every communication and confidence trick I've developed both in the corporate space and as an internationally recognized content creator.

As I sat down with a coffee in hand to write this conclusion, I felt like something was missing. As you can imagine, I did what I always do when I need advice: I called my mom. I sat on FaceTime with her and said, "I don't know how to describe what I think is missing. If I was twenty and reading this, honestly I think I would need a hug and a pep talk. Someone to tell me I'm going to figure this whole thing out." Because having everything you'll need for your career laid out in front of you is incredible, but it's also kind of scary.

So here's the letter I would write as a pep talk to my younger self and to you. I hope it feels like a warm hug at the end of our time together, because if there's one feeling I want to leave you with, it's that I believe in you.

Dear younger me,

Everyone says your twenties are the navigation years, and that must be true, because I felt lost throughout most of mine. But in being lost, there is so much I found out.

First, I found out that being an adult is kind of terrifying. I would be lying to you if I said that the fear of making the wrong decision or not measuring up ever really goes away. You'll probably always have waves of doubt that you aren't good enough, qualified enough, or deserving enough. You'll still have sweaty palms before interviews and occasional dread when you inevitably make a mistake. But with practice, you'll realize the fear you feel is there because you care. How powerful is that? Be scared, and do it anyway. Be terrified to apply for the job, take on the promotion, ask for time off, advocate for yourself, quit, or start your life over . . . and do it anyway. If it scares you, it's usually a sign you need to do it. The more things you do even though you're scared, the smaller the feeling becomes.

I also found out that most things don't matter, really. How freeing is that? It may sound dark and lonely, but it's quite the opposite. I learned that everyone is so caught up in their own journeys that they don't have any time to pay attention to yours. No one is looking at you funny or overanalyzing what you say, especially at work. So let the overthinking go. You're doing just fine.

I realize that the work you're doing may feel like the most important thing in the world today, but it probably won't matter five years from now. Neither will that mistake you made, bridge you burned, or rejection you faced. In fact, the only thing you'll regret is how hard you were on yourself for being imperfect. You'll realize that the mistakes that felt like mountains were in fact molehills all along. And actually, the mistakes were so small that today, you couldn't remember them even if you tried. It may feel like your whole world, but it's just a job.

I found out that having boundaries doesn't make you selfish, it makes you healthy. You can't light yourself on fire to keep others warm.

In all the lost that I was, I found out that you'll always figure shit out. Every rejection, roadblock, and heartbreak led me back to the ultimate truth: *You are always going to be OK.* You have a 100 percent success rate of surviving every bad day you've ever had. So as you evolve and things feel heavy, please remember: You're always going to figure it out, because you always have. I trust you. Be crazy enough to believe that you can accomplish every single thing you want. It takes just as much delusion to imagine the worst-case scenario as it does the best-case one.

Above all, I need to tell you that the career you build is an important part of you, but it isn't *you.* You won't be on your deathbed wishing you accomplished more from your cubicle. You won't be yearning for more late nights answering emails. You won't be reaching for the hand of the shareholder as you take your last breath. You'll be yearning for real connection. For memories. You'll be spending those last moments reflecting on a life well lived. Because your job is just a fucking job. It is the least interesting thing about you, and it will never, *ever* love you back.

So, yes, chase the big dreams. But remember the only thing in this world that deserves your unwavering loyalty and empathy is you. You're the boss. You can get ahead without losing your mind.

Thank you for being here with me.

xoxo,
Emily

ACKNOWLEDGMENTS

To my mom and dad—for a girl who just wrote a book, there will never be enough words to express my love and gratitude. Thank you for supporting my every ambition, rejection, and celebration. Because of you, I grew up in a home where I believed I could accomplish *anything.* I grew up in a home where my parents told me I was smart, powerful, and worthy. I recognize how much of a blessing that is.

Mom, thank you for sitting in front of our family computer for hours at a time, transcribing "books" that I was writing as a small girl. Dad, thank you for being my ultimate mentor, adviser, and rock—I have never been scared to take up space, because you have always reminded me not to shrink. You both are my best friends.

To my family (both by blood and chosen). You have poured into me and this work in ways I will always cherish. Whether sharing ideas, feedback, or *good luck* texts, you have always been in my corner. Thank you for being my anchors, safe spaces, and sources of belly laughs in between long days of writing.

To the best boss I've ever had, Reiss. Thank you. I don't know how I would have balanced full-time recruitment and this work without your support.

To Ginger Bertrand and Michele Yeo, my managers/advocates/champions—we did it. Thank you for betting on me and taking a chance on a twenty-four-year old kid posting recruitment tips on Instagram. Your guidance and support have meant everything to me.

To the incredible team at Tarcher, thank you for investing so much into *Clock In* and, frankly, for giving me the opportunity to bring these pages to life. This book would not exist without you.

And finally, so close to my heart is every single person who trusted me to support them on their career path. This platform is a gift and a privilege. Thank you.

NOTES

Chapter 1: Wake Up, the Dream Isn't Yours

4 **In fact, a startling:** Megan Cerullo, "More than Half of College Graduates Are Working in Jobs That Don't Require Degrees," *CBS News,* February 23, 2024, https://www.cbsnews.com/news/college-grads-jobs-underemployed/.

5 **In 2024, only about:** National Science Foundation, "Women, Minorities, and Persons with Disabilities in Science and Engineering: 2024," accessed June 30, 2025, https://ncses.nsf.gov/pubs/nsf24321/.

6 **Studies suggest that about:** YouthInsight (Student Edge), "Youth perceptions and attitudes to STEM," *STEM Equity Monitor: Primary and Secondary School Data,* Department of Industry, Science and Resources (Australia), 2023–24, https://www.industry.gov.au/publications/stem-equity-monitor/primary-and-secondary-school-data/youth-perceptions-and-attitudes-stem.

6 **A study conducted by UCLA and:** "Myth of Male 'Superior Math Ability' Hinders Female Students' Math Performance," Association for Psychological Science, September 27, 2023, https://www.psychologicalscience.org/news/2023-september-female-students-math-performance.html.

7 **A Microsoft study shows:** Holly Boothroyd, "How the Power of Community Is Crucial in Achieving Gender Balance in STEM," Impakter, September 26, 2019, https://impakter.com/how-the-power-of-community-is-crucial-in-achieving-gender-balance-in-stem-stemettes/.

7 **But only roughly 8 percent:** Anthony Martinez and Cheridan Christnacht, "Women Making Gains in STEM Occupations but Still Underrepresented," U.S. Census Bureau, January 26, 2021, https://www.census.gov/library/stories/2021/01/women-making-gains-in-stem-occupations-but-still-underrepresented.html.

8 **Thousands of people online:** Megan Rose Dickey, "#ILookLikeAnEngineer Aims to Spread Awareness About Diversity in Tech," TechCrunch, August 3, 2015, https://techcrunch.com/2015/08/03/ilooklikeanengineer-aims-to-spread-awareness-about-gender-diversity-in-tech/.

14 **The American Psychiatric Association:** Harvard Graduate School of Education, October 24, 2023, "Mental Health Challenges of Young Adults Illuminated in New Report," https://www.gse.harvard.edu/ideas/news/23/10/mental-health-challenges-young-adults-illuminated-new-report.

19 **In fact, Boston Consulting:** Gabrielle Novacek, "An Inclusive Workplace Is Good for Business," June 27, 2024, https://www.bcg.com/publications/2024/an-inclusive-workplace-is-good-for-business.

Chapter 2: Untying Your Identity from Work

26 **It's not shocking that:** Drew DeSilver, "The Concerns and Challenges of Being a U.S. Teen: What the Data Show," *Pew Research Center (Short Reads)*, February 26, 2019, https://www.pewresearch.org/short-reads/2019/02/26/the-concerns-and-challenges-of-being-a-u-s-teen-what-the-data-show/.

27 **Historically, many last names:** "It's a Living: Last Names That Started as Jobs," Merriam-Webster.com, accessed July 21, 2025, https://www.merriam-webster.com/wordplay/last-name-occupations-jobs-meaning.

28 **In fact, 50 percent:** "Job Unhappiness Is at a Staggering All-Time High, According to Gallup," CNBC, August 12, 2022, https://www.cnbc.com/2022/08/12/job-unhappiness-is-at-a-staggering-all-time-high-according-to-gallup.html.

29 **There are nearly 120,000:** J. Goh, J. Pfeffer, and S. A. Zenios, "The relationship between workplace stressors and mortality and health costs in the United States," *Management Science* 62, no. 2 (2015): 608–628.

39 **After all, 96 percent:** "Science of Fashion: How Different Clothes Make Us Feel," Icewear, accessed July 21, 2025, https://icewear.is/en-US/blog/science-of-fashion-how-clothing-changes-our-mood.

40 **The National Science Foundation:** Rebecca Strong, "How Many Thoughts Do We Have Per Day?" Healthline, last updated July 11, 2023, https://www.healthline.com/health/how-many-thoughts-per-day#thoughts-per-day.

40 **Of those thoughts, 80:** Nancy Colier, "Negative Thinking: A Dangerous Addiction," *Psychology Today,* April 8, 2019, https://www.psychologytoday.com/us/blog/inviting-monkey-tea/201904/negative-thinking-dangerous-addiction.

Chapter 3: The Hunt

58 **In fact, a recent:** Max Witynski, "Hiring Discrimination: The Problem That Won't Go Away," Northwestern Now, February 1, 2023, https://news.northwestern.edu/stories/2023/02/hiring-discrimination-the-problem-that-wont-go-away/.

58 **Unsurprisingly, applicants of color:** Witynski, "Hiring Discrimination."

59 **This study was re-created:** Patrick Kline, Evan K. Rose, and Christopher R. Walters, "A Discrimination Report Card," Becker-Friedman Institute for Economics, April 8, 2024, accessed via BFI PDF.

59 **Gender, age, and other:** Natalie Spievack, Urban Institute, "For People of Color, Employment Disparities Start Early," Urban Wire, accessed July 1, 2025, https://www.urban.org/urban-wire/people-color-employment-disparities-start-early.

59 **The truth is, white:** McKinsey & Company, "Race in the Workplace: The Black Experience in the US Private Sector," February 21, 2021, https://www.mckinsey.com/featured-insights/diversity-and-inclusion/race-in-the-workplace-the-black-experience-in-the-us-private-sector.

60 **For example, Black employees:** McKinsey & Company, "Race in the Workplace."

61 **Interestingly, women tend to:** Tara Sophia Mohr, "Why Women Don't Apply for Jobs Unless They're 100% Qualified," *Harvard Business Review,* August 25, 2014, https://hbr.org/2014/08/why-women-dont-apply-for-jobs-unless-theyre-100-qualified.

Chapter 4: Apply Yourself

87 **Over one billion people:** Maddy Osman, "Mind-Blowing LinkedIn Statistics and Facts (2025)," Kinsta, April 18, 2025, https://kinsta.com/blog/linkedin-statistics/.

Chapter 5: Make Your Network Work

96 **Referrals are often more:** Rachel Feintzeig, "Landing a Job Is All About Who You Know (Again)," *The Wall Street Journal,* February 13, 2023, https://www.wsj.com/lifestyle/careers/networking-job-search-c6f06b0c; Julia Freeland Fisher, "How to Get a Job Often Comes Down to One Elite Personal Asset," CNBC, December 27,

2019, https://www.cnbc.com/2019/12/27/how-to-get-a-job-often-comes-down-to-one-elite-personal-asset.html.

106 **Almost 80 percent of:** Julia Fisher, "How to Get a Job Often Comes Down to One Elite Personal Asset."

Chapter 6: Interview Boot Camp

113 **Fifty percent of employers:** Mary Lorenz, "1 in 2 Employers Know About a Candidate Within First 5 Minutes," CareerBuilder, August 2016, https://resources.careerbuilder.com/news-research/1-in-2-employers-know-about-a-candidate-within-first-5-minutes.

Chapter 7: Act Like It

137 **Nearly 70 percent of adults:** Abigail Abrams, "Yes, Impostor Syndrome Is Real. Here's How to Deal With It," *Time*, June 20, 2018, https://time.com/5312483/how-to-deal-with-impostor-syndrome/; "Study Finds 75% of Female Execs Experience Imposter Syndrome," *Los Angeles Business Journal*, July 3, 2023, https://labusinessjournal.com/business-journal-events/study-finds-75-of-female-execs-experience-imposter-syndrome/.

137 **Unsurprisingly, rates of reported:** Sheryl Nance-Nash, "Why Imposter Syndrome Hits Women and Women of Colour Harder," BBC Worklife, July 24, 2020, https://www.bbc.com/worklife/article/20200724-why-imposter-syndrome-hits-women-and-women-of-colour-harder.

139 **"Fake it till you":** Daryl J. Bem, "Self-Perception: An Alternative Interpretation of Cognitive Dissonance Phenomena," *Psychological Review* 74, no. 3 (May 1967): 183–200.

142 **Words actually account for:** James Carrier, "Mehrabian's 7-38-55 Communication Model: It's More Than Words," World of Work, July 2019, https://worldofwork.io/2019/07/mehrabians-7-38-55-communication-model/.

Chapter 9: Be Greedy

172 Studies show that individuals: Cheryl Robinson, "Hidden Cost of Not Negotiating: $1.5 Million in Lost Career Earnings," *Forbes*, April 8, 2025, https://www.forbes.com/sites/cherylrobinson/2025/04/08/hidden-cost-of-not-negotiating-15-million-in-lost-career-earnings/.

172 Additionally, a study conducted: "10 Salary Negotiation Quotes That Will Inspire You to Ask for a Raise," Payscale, accessed July 22, 2025, https://www.payscale.com/career-advice/10-salary-negotiation-quotes-will-inspire-ask-raise.

Chapter 11: Preserving Your Sanity

207 "In the 1990s and": Isabella Rosario, "When the 'Hustle' Isn't Enough," *Code Switch*, April 3, 2020, https://www.npr.org/sections/codeswitch/2020/04/03/826015780/when-the-hustle-isnt-enough.

210 The World Health Organization: "Burn-out an 'Occupational Phenomenon': International Classification of Diseases," World Health Organization, May 28, 2019, https://www.who.int/news/item/28-05-2019-burn-out-an-occupational-phenomenon-international-classification-of-diseases.

211 Studies show that productivity: Bob Sullivan, "Working More than 50 Hours a Week Makes You Less Productive," CNBC, January 26, 2015, https://www.cnbc.com/2015/01/26/working-more-than-50-hours-makes-you-less-productive.html.

INDEX

ABOUT THE AUTHOR

Emily Durham, better known as Emily the Recruiter, is a recruiter turned career coach and content creator. On her popular social media accounts and her podcast, *Clock In,* she gives real-world advice to help people thrive in their careers. Her work has been featured on *Good Morning America, BBC News,* in the *Globe and Mail,* and more. She lives in Toronto.

SHEN
and Neighboring
Kingdoms
Wei
魏
Er-cheng
River Li
Wu
Ying's
Village
MOUNT TAI
Donghai
Sea
Ying
應